Fre<

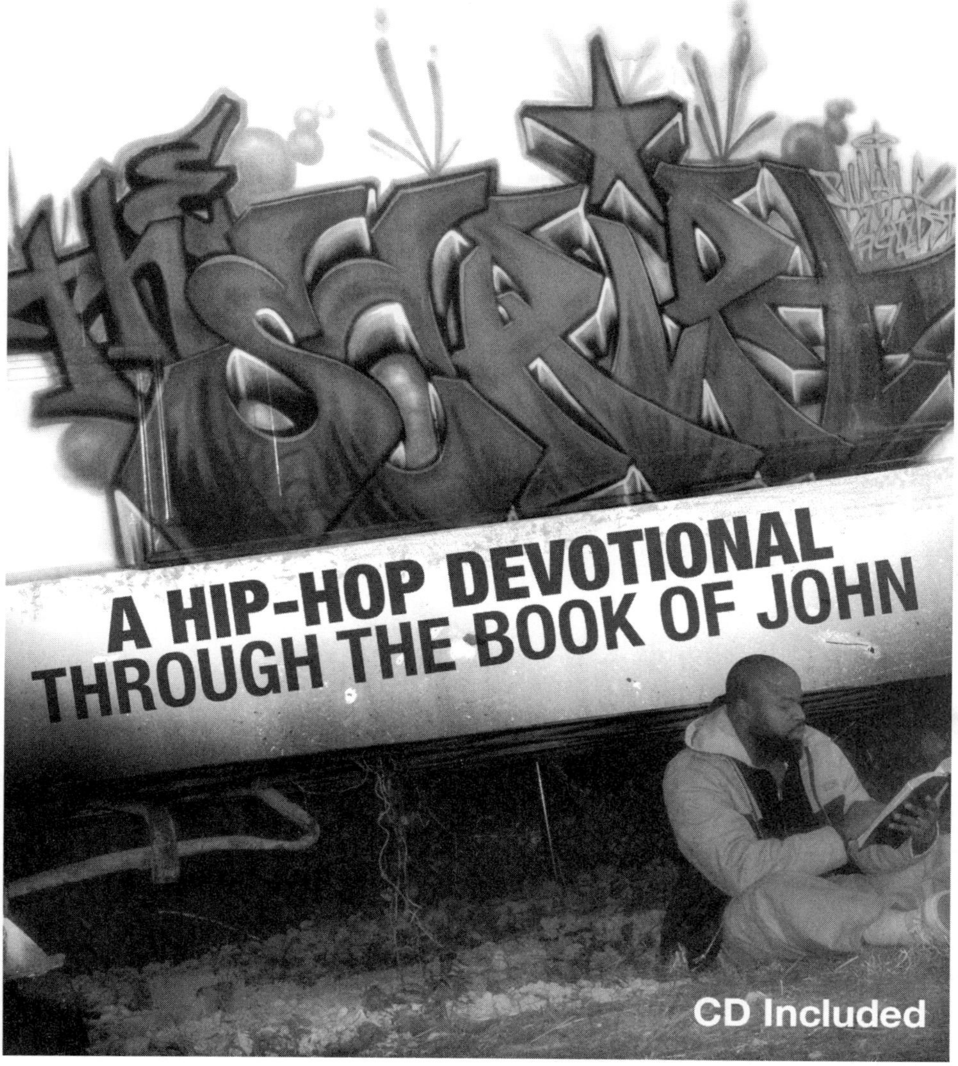

A HIP-HOP DEVOTIONAL THROUGH THE BOOK OF JOHN

CD Included

 youth specialties

The Script: A Hip-Hop Devotional Through the Book of John
Copyright 2008 by Fred D. Lynch III

Youth Specialties products, 300 S. Pierce St., El Cajon, CA 92020 are published by Zondervan, 5300 Patterson Ave. SE, Grand Rapids, MI 49530.

ISBN 978-0-310-27806-1

All rights reserved. No part of this publication may be reproduced, stored in a retrieval system, or transmitted in any form or by any means — electronic, mechanical, photocopy, recording, or any other — except for brief quotations in printed reviews, without the prior permission of the publisher.

Web site addresses listed in this book were current at the time of publication. Please contact Youth Specialties via e-mail (YS@YouthSpecialties.com) to report URLs that are no longer operational and replacement URLs if available.

Cover design by SharpSeven Design
Interior design by Mark Novelli, IMAGO MEDIA

Printed in the United States of America

08 09 10 11 12 • 20 19 18 17 16 15 14 13 12 11 10 9 8 7 6 5 4 3 2 1

CONTENTS

Introduction	4
Day 1—The Beginning: Finding Forever...Ever	8
Day 2—The Annunciation: Ring the Alarm	12
Day 3—The Wedding & Temple: Showstopper	16
Day 4—Nicodemus: Born Never to Die Again	20
Day 5—John the Baptist: Fade to Black	24
Day 6—Woman at the Well, Part One: No Matter the Dirt	28
Day 7—Woman at the Well, Part Two: Duped by Our Sin...Again	32
Day 8—Jesus and the Nobleman: No Love at Home	36
Day 9—Jesus and the Lame Man: Wanna Step Up?	38
Day 10—Bethsaida Confrontation: Can't Hold Back	42
Day 11—Jesus Feeds 5,000: A Touch of Heaven	46
Day 12—Capernaum Confrontation, Part One: Jesus Can't Be Played	50
Day 13—Capernaum Confrontation, Part Two: Losing Jesus in the Argument	54
Day 14—Capernaum Confrontation, Part Three: Marking the Sellouts	58
Day 15—Back to Jerusalem, Part One: Heavenly Credentials	62
Day 16—Back to Jerusalem, Part Two: Love Is Loud	66
Day 17—Back to Jerusalem, Part Three: Caught in the Act	70
Day 18—Jesus with the Jerusalem Believers: The Truth about the Truth	74
Day 19—Man Born Blind, Part One: Seeing for the Very First Time	78
Day 20—Man Born Blind, Part Two: Eyes Wide Shut	82
Day 21—Jesus the Good Shepherd: The Master's Metaphors	86
Day 22—Jerusalem Confrontation: Challenging the Master	90
Day 23—Lazarus Is Dead: A Time to Die	94
Day 24—Jesus with Mary and Martha: The Sting of Death	98
Day 25—Leaders React to a Resurrected Lazarus: Power Schemes	102
Day 26—Jesus' Triumphal Entry: Look Who's Back	106
Day 27—Jesus Is Sought Out by the Greeks: R.E.S.P.E.C.T.	110
Day 28—Jesus' Last Public Offer: The Outcry	114
Day 29—Jesus Washes the Disciples' Feet: Service from the Master	118
Day 30—Jesus Predicts His Betrayal: I Know Who's Hating	122
Day 31—Jesus Comforts His Own, Part One: No Heart Trouble	126
Day 32—Jesus Comforts His Own, Part Two: The Comforter	130
Day 33—Jesus Is the True Vine: Stay Connected	134
Day 34—Jesus Prepares the Disciples for His Departure: When I Leave, He Will Come	138
Day 35—Jesus Explains His Mission Plainly: Now You See It	142
Day 36—Jesus' High Priestly Prayer: Father, I Have a Dream	146
Day 37—Jesus Is Arrested: Sold Out with a Kiss	150
Day 38—Jesus before the Authorities: Truth on Trial	154
Day 39—Jesus before Pilate: Truth Is Slain in the Street	158
Day 40—The Crucifixion: Creation Hangs Creator on a Tree	162
Day 41—The Resurrection: Happy Endings	166
Day 42—Ascension: New Beginnings	172

INTRODUCTION

HOW TO USE *THE SCRIPT*

You can just read the verses and passages like you would a great novel—or you can follow along with the accompanying disc and listen to the musical tracks while you're reading them on these pages.

You can read *The Script* devotionally, too, checking out portions of the Gospel of John each day over the course of 42 days—that's how the book is divided up.

But *The Script* is more than just a hip-hop translation of Scripture! Don't forget that along with verses you can dig in and explore deeper questions. For instance:

> I provided a sidebar of word definitions and explanations called **Say What?** at the end of many of the 42 passages. Make sure you get a look at this—it's amazing the power and multiple meanings that words carry.
>
> If you do decide to read *The Script* devotionally, I wrote a **Devotional** after each of the 42 passages. You can read a mini-commentary on the passage and journal and answer the questions provided (go ahead—write directly on the page if you want!).
>
> Finally, there's the **Breathe Out** exercise. Check out the following suggestions for making the most of Breathe Out.

BREATHE OUT CONCEPT

Each day an assignment is given to reinforce what you learned (breathed in). The assignments are simple and should take three to five minutes. Since this is a six-week program, the assignment categories repeat over consecutive days (days one through seven times six weeks). The assignments reflect things done in hip-hop culture to capture your hip-hop heart and mind.

> Day 1: Write It (reflectively journal)
>
> Day 2: Tag It (make graffiti or draw out, illustrate, and compare)
>
> Day 3: Speak It (creatively compose in spoken-word form)
>
> Day 4: Rap It (make up your own rap lyrics)
>
> Day 5: Remix It (interpret)
>
> Day 6: Flip It (discover)
>
> Day 7: Go to God (pray)

Other breathe out ideas

- Journal about a time when God's love surprised you and made your day.
- Go to God and ask him to surprise you with his love this week.
- Draw five faces surrounding Jesus at a temple and what they probably looked like as he was preaching a passage.
- Journal about the first time you experienced embarrassment for the sake of truth.
- Imagine a visitor from another town coming and witnessing a surprising event from the week's Scripture. Write out a freestyle spoken-word (non-rhyming) piece about that visitor explaining the event to his friends when he gets home.

WHY ANOTHER NEW VERSION OF SCRIPTURE?

Language changes. New words are formed. Old words take on new meanings. Every generation needs to keep the language of the gospel message current, fresh, and understandable—the way it was for its very first readers. That's what *The Script* accomplishes for today's readers and hearers.

The Gospel of John was originally written in koiné Greek. That was the language of the common people. Today we'd call it "ghetto" Greek. Why was the most important message of all time written in such a simple language? So it could be transferred to people easily and accurately. There were no misunderstandings due to "canonically correct" traditional writing styles that most people were unfamiliar with. As a result, the gospel spread like wildfire.

Today many people enjoy reading and memorizing, for example, the King James Version of the Bible because of its poetic flow. Others enjoy versions that offer close, word-for-word translations from the original languages to English. *The Script* is designed to be "experienced." In other words, it brings to life the spirit of the original manuscripts that can get played down in formal English translations (e.g., the rhythm of the voices, the flavor of the idiomatic expressions, the subtle connotations of meaning) and brings it home for today's teenage reader through the infusion of hip-hop culture and language.

DOES *THE SCRIPT* USE EBONICS?

No. While there is hip-hop flavor and the use of urban slang for accent points in the rhyme schemes, *The Script* employs a great deal of contemporary language and touchstones in order to provide greater overall understanding for teenage readers. *The Script* actually represents a conscious attempt to move away from the use of Ebonics.

Instead of sacrificing the continuity of thought from the original text for street cred, *The Script* bends the powerful descriptive language of the street to tell the honest tale of Scripture.

HOW MUCH OF *THE SCRIPT* IS DRIVEN BY SLANG?

We sought to develop a classical style of literature with *The Script*, not a slang-driven work. As already noted, the colloquialisms in *The Script* are more or less widespread in mainstream culture; but also we wanted to avoid the overuse of subcultural slang that marginalizes. Of course, slang and even socially descriptive words change over time. Which is why we went to great lengths to develop *The Script* in a way that recaptures the passion and potency of the unchanging truth of God's Word in a language that teenagers use today. When looking at classic hip-hop, you find songs that employ serious poetry—of the street or otherwise—and have become timeless: "Rapper's Delight" by The Sugar Hill Gang (1979), "The Message" by Grandmaster Flash and the Furious Five (1982), "I Ain't No Joke" by Eric B. & Rakim (1986), "Nothin' but a G Thang" by Dr. Dre and Snoop Dogg (1992), and "Jesus Walks" by Kanye West (2004) all capture the cultural climates of their eras, but also transcend time and still speak to kids today—and will speak to future generations. And although we don't endorse all the lyrics in the aforementioned songs, the timelessness of these tunes is beyond question. And that's our hope for *The Script*.

The Script is a work of literature that reflects the truth of two major realities: The unchanging human condition and the constantly changing cultural conditions of our world.

RAP IS SO TRENDY; WILL *THE SCRIPT* BECOME OUT OF DATE?

The Script is part of a massive, growing culture that's long since taken the world by storm—hip-hop. It's not going anywhere fast. But as stated previously, even the meaning behind some hip-hop words can change over time. Which is why we didn't rely solely on hip-hop terms to get our points across; we also employed unchanging truths from the emerging culture, as well as phrasing from several different Bible versions.

With actual rappers communicating Scripture the way they would say it within their "emerging" culture, you capture a more potent and credible communication of truth.

WHAT'S SO DIFFERENT ABOUT *THE SCRIPT*?

It's not meant to replace your current Bible version of choice. Rather, it's designed as an interactive Bible paraphrase that can give you a fresh perspective on familiar phrases and passages through hip-hop "accents" and thoughtful, innovative use of contemporary language that will open your eyes and your mind. It's a smooth, easy read—even educational. (Check out the many sidebars that break down words that may be new to you—even familiar words are unpacked and discussed based on meanings you may not have considered yet.)

HOW CLOSE OF A TRANSLATION IS *THE SCRIPT* TO THE BIBLE?

The Script is a paraphrase of the Gospel of John that translates thought and tone—i.e., it's not a word-for-word translation. However, its construction was achieved through a meticulous process of analyzing an average of seven to 12 versions of Scripture for every verse you read in *The Script*. (Translations consulted include: The Message, The Living Bible, Contemporary English Version, New International Version, Today's New International Version, King James Version, Revised Standard, New American Standard, and several others.)

This is why you'll see, for example, "old" words from the King James Version and "new" words from the Contemporary English Version side by side in a synoptically postmodern flow that drives the point home stylistically without sacrificing the substance of Holy Scripture.

WHAT WILL I GET FROM *THE SCRIPT*?

Through the use of rhythm and rhyme you'll receive a deeper "visual" comprehension of the gospel. In other words, you'll perceive passages as whole units of thought. You'll also be able to memorize Scripture much more easily and thereby apply it to your life much more easily. As you encounter passages you've read hundreds of times before, it will be like reading them for the first time. Scripture will seem more alive and understandable as you experience the excitement of the gospel in the same way its first readers experienced it.

—Fred Lynch

DAY 1
THE BEGINNING: FINDING FOREVER...EVER

MOOD: MYSTICAL

JOHN 1:1-28

1 In the beginning was the Word, the manifest logic of God heard unblurred shining from the inner sanctum of the third.

2 Unbroken catastrophical quotes spoken from the essence of eternity's original notion.

3 All things were made by his motion and without him was no thing brought to being—all matter engrossed him.

4 In him was life, and that life was the Light of men

5 shining in the dark, but darkness didn't comprehend.

6 There was a man whose name was John—he was the God-send,

7 sent to point men to the Light that on sight they might enter in.

8 John himself was not the Light, just sent to represent

9 tha true illuminati that's kissed the face of everybody in this world coming or going, ignorant or knowing.

10 He was in the world, alive and growing, and though he made it all, they slept on him and kept on going.

11 He even came to his chosen, and his own kin closed him out and dissed 'im like he was an omen.

12 But to as many as would get wide-open and believe that he was just who he'd told 'em—to them he "spoke-in" the power to become God's child,

13 who were formed God-style...in full denial of any human medium—no flesh, blood, or brainstorm conceivin' 'em, strictly God born.

14 And the Word became flesh and manifested in our midst. And we beheld him at his best, a style that none could counterfeit. And we knew God had come down, like Father, like Son now: True from beginnin' to tha end, good from tha inside out.

15 (John knew what was up; he pointed him right out of the crowds—shouted to the people all around out loud, "Hear me now! This is the man I've been talking 'bout! I told y'all that one day soon he was comin' out. The original top billa; see I was just the temporary opening filla.")

16 But now he goin' fill ya 'cause he's stepping onto the stage, and we all gonna feel him blaze and catch grace for grace for grace.

17 See, Moses brought them laws and rules, but grace and truth came through the Messiah who is called Yeshua.

18 Now no man ever seen God's face and lived to tell about it. The only Son is the exception, straight outta heaven, immaculate from conception: It's the one-of-a-kind direct God expression whose confession is valid!

19 Now the priest & the temple assistants sent by the Jews from Jerusalem came way-long distance just to feel John out, test his clout—so they asked him who he claimed to be.

20 John straight-up told and flabbergasted them, "I'm not Christ. I know you're lookin'."

21 They got shooken, so they said, "What then, you Elijah or the Prophet?" And he said, "Not them."

22 "Then who? We're here to investigate this and must have answers, so speak up for yourself; stop dancing around the issue & enhance us."

23 "I be the voice in the wild places, like Isaiah says, 'Move out the road; the Lord's coming through—so make this path the straightest.'"

24 These interrogators from the Pharisees' sect were so frustrated from his statements

25 that they tried to bait him in: "If you're not Eli, or the Prophet, or the Christ, why you baptizin' then?"

26 John hit 'em back without retreating: "I baptize with water those believing, but One is sitting in front of you, and you still can't see him!

27 "He's reason—the One for which I forerun, promised to come—exploding after my season's done. See, in comparison I'm not worthy to untie his shoes."

28 This was John's confrontation with the Jerusalem Jews; it all went down east of Jordan, the baptizing spot that John used to use.

SAY WHAT?

John 1:1—The Greek translation for "word" is *logos*. That's where we get the word *logic*. John was letting us know that from the beginning, God's logic has been at work and caused everything in creation to shift into alignment with the very thoughts of God: "Let there be!"

DEVOTIONAL

Jesus Christ is the true Light, brighter than the night I'm in.

From our viewpoint this universe is a big mystery; but when God began his creation, God spoke exactly what he had in mind: nothing more, nothing less. Dominated by darkness the whole of creation was moved by the cadence of God's command: "Light!" Light is movement, light is energy, and light is radiance uncontained and unable to stop. When Jesus "moves into the neighborhood," John says his very presence is like turning on the light—not just any light, but the Light. The same Light that had helped make it all is now here to shine. Think about the moment just before the Light came on. What would that type of void feel like? Cold...dark...alone...then—bam! There was Light.

There was Light!

- How would you describe your life before you sensed the warmth of God's light?

- Describe the anticipation of a soul waiting for the light of God to shine on it.

- How do you feel now when you face the unknown, knowing God's in control of your life?

BREATHE OUT: WRITE IT

Journal about the first time you sensed God speaking to you.

DAY 2
THE ANNUNCIATION: RING THE ALARM

MOOD: ELECTRIC

JOHN 1:29-51

29 The next day John saw Jesus walking through a sea of souls and said, "BEHOLD! The Lamb of God sent to pay sin's toll for the world on a whole!

30 "This is the One of whom I used to say that, 'Once I scat, then comes the top act that's from way back.'

31 "And I didn't know who he was—I can't brag; I have to face facts—but God told me to go & baptize & that's where he'd step on stage at."

32 John put it down & said, "I knew it was him when I saw the Spirit descending & flew upon him.

33 "Just who he was I didn't have a clue until then, but he who sent me baptizing had this rendezvous planned. He said to 'stay high post & watch me close for the clue that I'm showing: The One you see my Spirit fall on & remain—that's my chosen. He baptizes with the Holy Ghost.'

34 "I saw & I know it! This is God's Son, the holy phenomenon, the only begotten one."

35 When the next day come, two disciples stood post with John...

36 ...and looking up caught sight of Jesus as he strolled on & he couldn't keep it in—he had to shout it out & told on 'em, "There he go! The Lamb of God, y'all—behold him!"

37 John's boys heard 'im say that, and it swayed 'em—straightway then they took after Jesus' pathway when...

38 ...Jesus swung around & saw that they was on his prey—& he asked them, "What you sayin'?" They said, "Master, where you stayin'?"

39 He said, "Alright right this way then" & they stayed in his den all day, parlayin' from about 10 in the a.m.

40 Now one of the two from John's crew that followed Jesus name was Andrew—Simon Peter was whom he was kin to.

41 So Drew first found brother Pete & began to blurt it: "We found the Messiah" (which is "Christ" interpreted, but that's how the Hebrews worded it).

42 He brought his brother to Jesus to meet him, so on the low he could self-observe it & Jesus, looking straight through Simon's tactics, switched prophetic & threw him off like a backflip when he read his mail like a transcript: "Don't say a word, kid; I know ya, son o' Jonas. Ya name is Simon, but I'm goin' complete ya & call you Peter when I'm done."

43 The day after, the Master wanted to go down to Galilee, and finding Philip, Jesus said to him, "Follow me."

44 And being from Bethsaida, the same town as Drew and P,

45 Phillip found Nathanael & said, "I got somebody you gotta see! We found the One that Moses & the prophets described to a T—Jesus, the son of Joseph, representin' them Nazarenes."

46 "Nazareth, ha!" Nathanael screamed, "What kinda scheme is you believin'? Them Nazarenes is straight ghetto!" Phillip said, "Well, you come & see then!"

47 And when Jesus seen 'em approachin', he started to boastin' on Nate: "Y'all lookin' at a for-real Israeli—ya feel me? Ain't nothin' about this brother fake."

48 Nathanael was like, "WHAT? Where you know me from?" Jesus was like, "Son, if you wantin' to quiz me, I saw you before Philip called you under the fig tree—is you diggin' me?"

49 Nate was surprised by the ability of the Lord's eyes & replied, "Rabbi, you're the King of these Israelis & the Son of the Most High."

50 So Jesus smiled, quizzed 'em back on a rhetorical style, "You simply believe because of my prophetic oracles now? You can start expecting full pictorials, child.

51 "I'm tellin' you, from this moment right here, right now, you goin' see 'the heavenly echelons revealin' they files & watch them angels ascend and descend upon the man child."

SAY WHAT?

John 1:39 — Do you ever think about how much time Jesus must have spent with his disciples in mere conversation? The first time Jesus connected with his first few followers must have been phenomenal. Think about it: Scripture says that they were with Jesus for a full day at the place he was staying. I would've loved to have been part of that conversation!

DEVOTIONAL

We need a revelation to get a revolution.

Revolution always begins with a revelation. The ability to see from the inside what's about to happen on the outside is released only to those bold enough to go beyond the norm; these are revolutionaries. Most people just play it safe and learn to deal with the way things are, but not revolutionaries. As dangerous as change can be, they see it coming and begin to ring the alarm. Revolution isn't always pretty, safe, or fun, but it's necessary. When Jesus "arrives," John the Baptist can only point and cry out, "Behold! [Look at him!] The Son of God who came to change the world!" Think about being there and dealing with the religious mess of that day: "How will we change more than 400 years of 'no voice from God'?" Look at him! "How will we see revival come back to God's people and restoration to a nation?" Look at him! "How will, when will, where will, who will...?" Look at him! Just look to Jesus, and all of those great questions can be answered — starting with revelation.

He rang the alarm.

- List three areas in your life in need of a revolution.

- When will you "ring the alarm" on these areas?

- How will you announce to proclaim that a change is coming?

BREATHE OUT: TAG IT

Tag (draw) an account of John pointing Jesus out to the crowd.

DAY 3
THE WEDDING & TEMPLE: SHOWSTOPPER

MOOD: SURPRISED

JOHN 2:1-25

1 Three days later was this wedding down in Cana; mother Mary participated,

2 plus Jesus & the discip'es came there.

3 Halfway through the gala they started to notice the wine was getting low, so Mary approached Jesus & told it: "You know they low on wine."

4 Jesus asked his moms, "Whose concern is that, yours or mine? Now's just not my time." "Fine."

5 But Mary went on anyway to the staff & instructed the crew, "Whatever he says, boo, I want you to do."

6 Standing barely outta view was six ceramic water pots used for sanitization rituals—simply habitual Jewish customs kept w/ pride by, like a fat medallion—each tub was about 25 gallons.

7 Jesus had 'em gather 'em and said, "Fill each pot w/ water." And they did it till each was at the brim.

8 "Now take a pitcher over to the master of the ceremony & tell him that was on me...and keep the party goin'."

9 So when the emcee took a sip of the water that was miraculously switched (not fully knowing the real, but his busboys knew the deal), he just tripped & called for the groom back to the room to speak on this liquid.

10 He said, "Man, you got me straight trippin' on this tonic; to be honest most folks serve their best stuff up front to astonish & after they've impressed the crowds, they bring the cheap coolers out—but you saved the best till now!"

11 This was the very first miracle in Galilee, where Jesus had 'em staggerin' at the glory he unsleeved & his whole set believed.

12 His disciples, moms & brethren—all following his lead—went down to Capernaum to retreat from the journey & you know how time flies when you ain't worryin'.

13 Like a flurry in came the Passover season, so Jesus went up to Jerusalem to celebrate in the city of peace-in'.

14 Soon as he stepped inside the temple region, the whole court was filled w/ fools teamed w/ demons acting straight heathen! Vendors selling doves, sheep, oxen right outta their carts; & like that wasn't goin' too far, the whole bazaar was run by loan sharks.

15 These fools were acting too bold, but now they pushed past the envelope. So Yeshu' went & got a rope that he made out of some leather, and putting together a strap, commenced to whipping heads right out the tabernac'. Sheep, doves & cattle all got tackled; every hustler, rogue, and rascal—Jesus cast their money out, too! (Ohh!)

16 And he told those who were selling doves & pigeons, "Get this ism outta my sight... makin' my Father's house a flea market—don't you ever try it!"

17 That's how he sparked it. And the disciples remembered David's prophetic remarks that "for zeal of God's house the Messiah would have mad heart."

18 "Now just who do you think you are?" the Jewish leaders stepped in, questionin'. "If God is with you, show us a miraculous sign to justify your aggression, man."

19 Jesus answered them, "All right then, break this temple down, and in three days I'll build it up again."

20 "Forty-six years to build this place & you can raise it up in three days? Your hostile ways must have you dazed!"

21 But Jesus spoke on the temple of his fleshly frame.

22 After he was resurrected, in retrospect they reflected & realized that Jesus had said it just as the Scriptures claimed!

23 From that Passover trip up to Jerusalem, so many were moved by him and believed on his name. Watching the miracles that Jesus displayed brought him mad fame.

24 Nevertheless, all the same Jesus played 'em close 'cause he knew how unpredictable & fickle the crowd goes.

25 He knew what men were really like & didn't need a seminar; so judging his popularity by polls was highly irregular.

SAY WHAT?

John 2:11—Scripture tells us that Jesus' entire family and his first few followers "believed" when they witnessed his first miracle. However, as we journey through the rest of the book of John, we see how it took some time for both his family (John 7:5) and his disciples (John 16:30) to fully grasp Jesus' identity. This shows us that belief is more of a spiritual journey than a mental destination.

John 2:22—The old adage says, "Hindsight is 20/20." It was only "after" Jesus rose from the dead that so many pieces of the puzzle fit into place for the disciples. This is why we must put our trust in God even when we can't tell what's coming around the corner—we'll discover that everything Jesus said is true!

DEVOTIONAL

Jesus is clued in to all your doings, but will you include him?

Walking in the footsteps of Jesus as a disciple was anything but predictable. One time they were at a wedding party, and he was miraculously creating more wine; the next they were at the temple, and he violently shut down the event all the while quoting Scripture to prove his point. Most preachers would've killed the party and opted for more church. Why would he keep the party going but crash the worship service? The celebration at the wedding was genuine, exciting, and full of the hope of new life while the celebration at the temple had stopped being about worship a long time ago; it had become a show. The religious leaders had plenty of things to get people ready to worship—they just left out the worship. How many things do we put in place of the one true thing God desires most? How many T-shirts, bumper stickers, Jesus bobbleheads, CDs—even devotionals—will we allow to trash up God's space and keep us distracted from building our house of prayer? Anything that's in the way of the Rabbi—he'll knock it over, run it out, disrupt all the seemingly good things taking up space that belongs to the Father.

Ordinary water pots

- How normal would you rate your life on a scale of one to 10? (one being "normal as can be" and 10 being "super extraordinarily unique")

- Jesus had these ordinary pots gathered together, filled up, and drawn out of to keep the wedding celebration going.
  — Who have you been "gathered together with"? (In other words, name two to four of your Christian friends.)

  — Have you been filled up lately? If so, how has Jesus filled you? (for example, with love, joy, peace…)

  — How is Jesus drawing you out to help someone around you?

- What things in your life are you willing to present to Jesus today so he can use them to help others?

BREATHE OUT: SPEAK IT

Write out a spoken-word-style poem about the disruption at the temple.

DAY 4
NICODEMUS: BORN NEVER TO DIE AGAIN

MOOD: WARM SUMMER'S NIGHT

JOHN 3:1-22

1. One evening Nicodemus, a Pharisee—that was a priestly Jewish VIP w/ status like a big celebrity—

2. came seeking Jesus on the low, discreetly saying, "Rabbi, you think very deeply, so teach me. Increasing my belief that you're God's elite is easy when I see these people receive your miraculous deeds."

3. Jesus said, "Unless a man has the spiritual eraser of a reborn nature, he can never see the kingdom of his Creator."

4. Nicodemus said, "What you're sayin' is foreign—when a man is old, how can he be reborn? Can he resume his place in his mother's womb and get re-formed?"

5. Jesus stepped beyond the norm and repeated himself with more emphasis: "Unless a man's entrance is born of water and Spirit, he's limited from stepping to the kingdom's premises, for instance.

6. "If it's born of flesh, it only begets a nest full of flesh; yet Spirit reflects Spirit—anything it connects with is blessed.

7. "So don't trip on the born-again script that I blaze; I didn't say this phrase to leave you astonished and amazed.

8. "The wind blows where it wants to, and you hear the way it flows, but its origin is undisclosed—where it goes is stealth mode. Everyone exposed to the Holy Spirit knows it's the same code for those who choose to have born-again souls."

9. Nicodemus had a look of amazement on his face. "This is hard to embrace. How can all of these things take place?"

10 Jesus told him, "You're supposed to be top scholar of the whole Hebrew race & it's a sad case that you can't even trace these facts that are basic.

11 "Now hear me stress this 'cause I've got to say it: Any subject we addressed is subjected to being visually tried and tested, and yet you treat our testimony messy & question it & y'all still not receptive to me—that's backwards & dyslexic.

12 "See, if you're a slow learner concerning my statements on the terra firma, how can you discern the heavenly terms in which I'm trying to turn ya onto?

13 "No man's ever gone to God's presence by ascending into heaven, except Immanuel, who was up there first and came down to dwell & be parallel.

14 "And just like Moses in the wilderness grabbed the serpent and raised it, in the same way the Son of Man has to be elevated.

15 "So whoever believes in him won't ever be terminated but instead would receive life that's eternally germinated.

16 "You want an accurate calculation of God's love for creation? Consider the weight of his only begotten Son being placed on earth's location & given as a donation for exoneration that whoever believes in him would live forever w/o expiration.

17 "For God sent not his Son to leave the world in condemnation but that all Homo sapiens experience the sensation of his embrace &

18 "catch exemption status from death & not even taste it—just like that. See, the opposite is quite toxic—not believing on God's only begotten Son will leave you rotten in your coffin w/ no options.

19 "See, I'm-a show you the real problem, so heed my caution: Men preferred the dark side, evil in their archives; the Light of life has arrived, yet most still strive & they opt for apartheid.

20 "Some hate the Light & just can't stand it...caught red-handed breaking commandments...sooner stay stranded in darkness than spark this truth that'll leave 'em reprimanded.

21 "On the other hand—it's the opposite spectrum—those who accept the Light & welcome God's inspection, striving to do what's right & reflect him: It's evidence of a divine connection."

22 After Jesus dropped this midnight lecture, he left Jerusalem for the Judean sector to rest there. It was less hectic, and the crowds were receptive, so the rabbi & his allies chose to reside & baptize there.

SAY WHAT?

John 3:12—*Terra firma* is Latin for the firm or solid earth, the ground upon which walk every day.

DEVOTIONAL

We must abandon the old way of getting life into our lives.

Every now and then Jesus would lift the veil between the natural and spiritual without the use of parables; he would just tell it like it is. And just as if someone turns on a light in the midst of creatures that thrive in the darkness, we would scatter in surprise and confusion at the light of Jesus' words. When Jesus speaks to Nicodemus, he utters words that shake the elderly Jewish teacher, and his words still shake us today. His word choices are truly classic; he uses terms such as being born again, ascension into heaven, the calculation of God's love, condemnation, and exemption from our deepest crisis—we actually like being separated from God. Yet he also gives assurance to Nicodemus' soul by unveiling the truth about the work of God: The fact we even have the notion of seeking God out is evidence of God working within us. Jesus came not only to disclose that evidence but also to blow the case wide-open. As wide as his arms could stretch—on the cross.

Here's the verdict.

- Jesus' "born again" quote really surprises Nicodemus. Find another quote from Jesus you find surprising or shocking and write it down.

- Jesus came and caught us in the act of separation from God but didn't condemn us; he still loves us. Give your own calculation of that love—how much does God's love mean to you?

- What part of your life can you look at and say, "This part of me has truly been born again"?

BREATHE OUT: RAP IT

Write out four rap lines that end by rhyming with the phrase "born again."

DAY 5
JOHN THE BAPTIST: FADE TO BLACK

MOOD: CALM

JOHN 3:23-36

23 John was up the river in Aenon holdin' classes close to Salim where the water was high, baptizing the masses. Multitudes of souls took this passage despite the traffic 'cause it stayed congested...

24 (back before John got arrested).

25 And just at that time a controversy started to brew between John's Taliban & certain established Jews on the practice of baptism—does it really make one pure? But this was just a contentious ploy for sure to lure John's men into debate, and some of his disciples took the bait.

26 Agitated at these religious ingrates, they approached John and said, "Sensei, you recall the other day at the Jordan the one who came to you & you proclaimed him the Lord? Well, now he's starting to draw numbers in abundance; it's getting redundant. If he keeps blowin' up like this, we're headed for sunset, and we don't feel we're done yet."

27 John sensed panic & calmed their hysteria. "I'm tellin' ya— there's really no need to worry here; and if he's blowing up like you say he is, then right in the middle of God's will is where we are & besides, no man of his own clout stands superior. If he's a cut above the rest, I suggest he's heaven blessed.

28 "You all can attest that I never said I was all that! 'Just the forerunner for the number-one Son o' wonders.'

29 "The one who gets to vow out the nuptials: See, that's the groom, but the best man is just happy to be in the same room & see true love bloom. In this my joy is full—just to see him jump that broom.

30 "His decibels have to be raised to the max, till volume is full blast. But I've got to fade to black.

31 "He who's from the throne is in a league of his own; can't compare the spiritual against the flesh & the bone. It's phantasm deeper than I could imagine or fathom 'cause we descended from Adam, so there's no crossing the chasm.

32 "But now then the holy Skywalker is talking, testifying what he's seen and heard—but man objects his words, treatin' his verbs like a tabloid plot.

33 "But he who sees his thesis and receives it has set his faith on lock that God is real—signed & sealed...is you feelin' me?

34 "God's emissary speaks his King's tongue in fluency—fluently w/o truancy or impunity is the Spirit measured out on him w/ all gratuity.

35 "You must see its mad affinity in the Trinity; and the Father's ordered all things to the Son—it's the dynasty of divinity.

36 "No amenities to this absolute truth: Believeth on the Son & it's done—death can't touch you. But such of you fools who refute & refuse his rules won't see the life of God, but the side that is cruel: You lose."

SAY WHAT?

John 3:25—The word *taliban* undoubtedly evokes many negative connotations, but did you know its original meaning in Arabic is "student" or "students"? This shouldn't surprise you; many words in the English language first meant for good also have been twisted around for negative purposes—so make sure you take regular peeks into the dictionary so you know the history behind the words you speak! In this verse, the context is "students"—those followers of John the Baptist who'd soon be introduced to the greatest Teacher ever.

DEVOTIONAL

"It was never about you." All that you do is for his purpose.

Good performers know how to make a memorable entrance onstage. The greatest performers, however, also know how to make a good exit. They can sense when it's time to step off the stage, even if it's while the crowd is crying out for more. John the Baptist recognizes his own curtain call is approaching after he introduces Jesus. The words he was no doubt born to shout—"Behold the Lamb of God!"—also mean, "It's my time to go now." John captures it when says, "He [Jesus] must increase, and I must decrease." John's able to let go of the spotlight because he's made peace with the full picture, realizing it was never really about him—but we're all here to do what we do and then move on. I'm sure John, at the end of his life, could look back and smile, saying, "I had only one chance—and I lived out loud with all of my heart, and I have no regrets."

Fade to black

- Can you identify anything in your life that might stop you from living with no regrets?

- When it's your time to fade to black, what type of memories would you like to leave?

- In which areas in your life do you sense that you must decrease and God must increase?

BREATHE OUT: REMIX IT

Write out John 3:27-30 in your own words. Describe three different emotions you can imagine John experiencing as he comes to this conclusion that it's his time to "fade to black." Then journal about a time when you've felt those same emotions.

DAY 6
WOMAN AT THE WELL, PART ONE: NO MATTER THE DIRT

MOOD: FUNKY ATTITUDE (DEFENSIVE)

JOHN 4:1-19

1 When the Lord knew it couldn't be denied that the Pharisees (you know the ones—religious eagle eyes) realized how the rumor rose that John hadn't baptized as many people's lives as the deified

2 (although Jesus didn't conduct the baptisms back then himself; he allowed his disciples to chip in and help),

3 that's when Jesus decided to leave Judea, going to Galilee

4 but needed to take a shortcut through Samaria.

5 Or should I say Samaria, a.k.a. Sychar, not much farther from Joseph's land inherited from Jacob, his father. Jesus sat down at the well, frazzled from his travels—about the sixth hour, according to the hourglass gravel.

6 And what in the world? Whoa—what do you know? A Samaritan woman came by to get some H_2O.

7 Jesus asked her, "Hey, can you get me some, too, yo?"

8 (Jesus' disciples had the munchies real deep, so they broke to go downtown to buy up some meat.)

9 The Samaritan woman said, "Wait a minute—how is it that you being a Jew have the nerve to ask me to get you a drink, too? You know the two don't have any dealings when it comes to Samaritans—y'all Jews have no feelings."

10 Jesus said, "If you only knew and could recognize God's gift & who it is asking you for a sip, you wouldn't have tripped; you would have flipped the script and asked for aqua from the author. He woulda turned around and gave you some living water."

11 The woman said, "You gots no rope or cable, bucket or label, plus the well is deep. I think you're Cain because you aint Abel. Now how you giving 'living' water for me to drink, child—whatcha saying?

12 "You think you're greater than my forefather Jacob who, by the way, gave us this well (in case you were baffled) and drank from it himself, plus his children and cattle."

13 Jesus said, "Whoever obeys their thirst and senses and drinks the type of water that this well dispenses will thirst again and again, never finished, as soon as their hydration diminishes.

14 "But whoever drenches their thirst in the water that I cleanse with will thirst no more from the core—mine eternally quenches. I'll place a well deep within ya, springing up life that forever replenishes."

15 The woman said, "I'm sold, so give me this water for my soul so I'll never have to come back to this hole."

16 Jesus said, "First go home and come back wit' cha hubby."

17 She said, "I never really had a man who proposed, who loved me." Jesus said, "You speak the truth about the lifestyle you practice.

18 "'Cause the five you've had is just been some cats that you shacked with."

19 Her jaw dropped with shock from the truth that flowed like faucet. She said, "From my perception I detect that you're a prophet."

SAY WHAT?

John 4:7—In ancient Jewish culture it was very odd for a rabbi to speak to a non-Jewish female, especially if the rabbi was alone (verse 8 says the disciples went to get some food). This actually looked like a very scandalous situation, because nine times out of 10 this woman would've thought, *This man is after more than just a drink of water*... If she thought that, she was right! Jesus was after the redemption of her soul. And because Jesus chose to enter into an awkward conversation, this woman's life was changed forever.

DEVOTIONAL

Jesus isn't fazed by our mess.

Has anyone ever come over to your house unexpectedly? You can feel really awkward if your place is a mess. What do you do—let her in or keep her standing outside while you do the 45-second clean-up drill? Jesus drops into the world of this Samaritan woman completely unexpected and unknown, and he immediately moves past the polite space we expect everybody to stay in. Instead he makes a beeline for the real issues of her heart: The messy, unresolved, and out-of-control issues. Jesus isn't thrown off by how messy our lives may be, nor is he deceived by the front we try to put up, making everybody think our lives are normal and clean. Jesus shows up in the most natural, messy, unreligious parts of our lives, and from there he wants to work. Jesus speaks about this woman's sin without surprise or disgust; it's just a matter of fact. But as he proceeds to describe what God can do for her, he blows her mind through the endless possibilities of what could be: Her thirst forever quenched, true worship, and everlasting life. It's enough to make you want to say, "Please, Jesus, come in—no matter the dirt!"

Excuse the mess.

- If you were having a conversation with Jesus, and he busted you by telling you all he knows about your messiest sins, what would you do?

- What's so special about the woman's quote that Jesus "knew all of her business," and why does that make her want to follow him?

- What do you think the disciples are thinking the whole time all this is taking place? Does the situation look messy to them?

BREATHE OUT: FLIP IT

List three "dirty" issues in your life Jesus wants to help you with, then share your story with a friend.

DAY 7
WOMAN AT THE WELL, PART TWO: DUPED BY OUR SIN...AGAIN

MOOD: FASCINATED

JOHN 4:20-42

20 "Well our fathers worshiped on this mountain back in the day, but you Jews say that Jerusalem's the place to worship and praise."

21 Jesus said, "The time is coming and the seconds are counting when you'll neither worship in Jerusalem or in this mountain.

22 "You see, you're clueless 'cause you worship an invisible image, yet we know because salvation started from Jewish lineage.

23 "But the new style's coming, starting now, for true worship recruits. The Father searches for the worship that's in Spirit and in truth.

24 "God's a Spirit; they that draw near in terms of endearment must exhibit worship that's in truth and in Spirit."

25 The woman said, "Well, Messiah's coming, and they call him the Christ; when he comes, tell us everything pertaining to life."

26 Jesus said, "It's no doubt that you're speaking from the Book—in fact, the One that you talking 'bout is the One that you're looking at."

27 And at that moment guess who walked in but his disciples. Surprised to see him trifle with this new female arrival, they all wanted to know why he was standing with this madam, but they wouldn't pop the question 'cause they didn't feel entitled.

28 The woman left the water pot because she felt so strongly about her experience, so she went & told her homies,

29 "Come to see a man who told me everything & if this isn't the Christ, then I don't know who is!"

30 Then all of the men from Samaria in the city came together and went out to Jesus like a committee.

31 At the same time the men were coming from downtown, the disciples were trying to get Jesus to chow down.

32 Jesus said, "Keep your meat 'cause right now I'm comfortable—besides, you didn't know I eat my own type of lunchables."

33 The disciples were like, "What? Did someone else come up and give Jesus some plate and cup off of their lunch truck?"

34 Jesus said to them, "The type of meat I eat is simply to finish all the work I'm doing for him who called and sent me.

35 "Don't say to yourself, 'In four months it's time for harvest.' Look close. The fields are white! The time is right. Forget who started.

36 "The reapers get paid and gather fruit that lives forever, so both the sower and the reaper can rejoice together.

37 "This is where we get the saying that's so accurate: 'One sows immaculate seeds, but others reap after it.'

38 "So now I've sent all of you out to get a paycheck from a place that you never even had to break a sweat."

39 From that set a lot of Samaritans believed from the witness of the woman testifying, "Jesus knew all my business!"

40 Now the Samaritans wanted to kick it and build, so Jesus agreed to hang out a couple o' days and chill.

41 Many more Samaritans believed in him when they heard the power of the Spirit that was packed in Jesus' word.

42 People all over the region told the woman, "Now we believe him for other reasons, not just for the things that you've been telling us that he's done—'cause since we've heard him preach some, it's like a beacon, and we know that he's the Christ, indeed: the one to bring the world its freedom."

SAY WHAT?

John 4:26—There were only a handful people to whom Jesus revealed he was the Messiah: A couple of fishermen, a man born blind (whom he healed), and this woman of questionable reputation. Jesus chose to let everyone else figure it out. What a privilege for those (like us) with "low status."

DEVOTIONAL

Sin never soothes the soul of its real problem.

Sin has always promised us something it could never give simply because it boasts of what it ain't got. Adam was promised a supreme knowledge to rival the Creator's; what he got was the death of his race and separation from God. Sin always takes you further than you want to go, gives you more than you want to have, and keeps you bound longer than you care to become enslaved. The woman at the well had a problem we all share: She'd been duped into believing her sin (adultery in her case) would soothe the deep hunger within her soul. We all experience the dilemma of getting duped by our sin, offering up the sacrifice of our very souls in exchange for the painful reality that sin isn't what our souls need to thrive. Jesus came on a mission to help us out with our deepest problem: Our worship problem.

In search of true worshipers

- When did you realize God was searching for you?

- If God is looking for true worship, then what is true worship?

- Why does true worship capture God's attention?

BREATHE OUT: GO TO GOD
Go to God and spend some time in uninterrupted worship.

DAY 8
JESUS AND THE NOBLEMAN: NO LOVE AT HOME

MOOD: FRUSTRATED

JOHN 4:43-54

43 Now after two days Jesus left Samaria and went to Galilee

44 (where there was barely a prophet of God who can ever expect to get into his own country and gain some respect).

45 But when he got to Galilee, his rep had already reached the Galileans who had seen his miracles at the feast.

46 Into Galilee now Jesus returned once again to the place of water-wine conversion. A certain nobleman was worried with concerns of his son who was sick back in Capernaum.

47 When he had heard the rumor that Jesus had left Judea to jet to Galilee, he went up to see him. Intercepting Jesus, he asked if he would accept the chance to come and heal his son who was nearly at the point of death.

48 So Jesus said to the man, "Now if you don't receive a sign and wonder that's visible, then you won't believe."

49 When the nobleman said, "Sir, would you please try to come down with me, or my child—will be deceased."

50 Jesus told him, "Leave; I've healed his infection." The man believed his words and went his own direction.

51 So as the man was walking home & then his butlers saw him on the corner, said, "Hey, your son recovered."

52 And so he asked him, "What time when the fever had left him?" They told him, "Yesterday right around seven."

53 So right away the father realized it was at the same time & hour Jesus said that "Your son is alive." It opened up the house keeper's eyes & the situation caused their faith in Christ to have deeper ties.

54 Now that was twice that the Christ decided to get fly displaying miracles in Galilee, leaving Judea.

DEVOTIONAL
Overcoming the frustration of indifference

Jesus has just come off an incredible trip from Samaria where his disciples have no doubt witnessed things way outside their normal, day-to-day routine. Now fired up with evidence that Jesus is a prophet, they all come back to Galilee and have to deal with people who still don't give him respect. Possibly one of Jesus' biggest frustrations on his mission was that his own people didn't get it. It's often the ones who see you every day who are the hardest to convince when you've changed because they've settled for sameness, and indifference blocks their view. You know you're different, but they can't see it; neither do they care. Frustrated over their smugness to stay in unbelief yet drawn by his love for them, Jesus heads back to his own people, and out of all surprises, he runs right into another opportunity to do what he came to do. Instead of letting frustration hold him back, he speaks words that spark faith and bring healing.

The man believed and went his way.

- Who are some people in your life who are so used to seeing the "natural" side of you that your spiritual aspect is often shrouded from them?

- Do you ever feel like you get shut down by the way people see you?

- What would it be like to step beyond the pain of disrespect and still give words to spark others' faith and bring healing?

BREATHE OUT: WRITE IT
Journal about the frustrations you face when people don't take you seriously.

DAY 9
JESUS AND THE LAME MAN: WANNA STEP UP?

MOOD: IMPROBABLE

JOHN 5:1-18

1. Soon after these matters, Jesus went back to Jerusalem because another feast of the Jews was on.

2. And in the city there were five ponds near this Sheep Gate—in the Hebrew tongue they would call it Bethsaida.

3. At the same place a whole gang o' sick folks would stay all day laying. The scene was amazing—blind, crippled & crazy all there waiting. What the pool held in it was more potent than minerals; they could wade in.

4. From what the old folks were sayin', there was an angel of the Lord that would pass that way certain seasons, making waves & stirring up the irrigation & the first patient that would touch the water would get healed w/o need of payment.

5. This one kid (an invalid) overdid it—he laid in the same spot 38 years, like it was a bid.

6. Jesus focused on this man stretched out, hurt & hopeless, asked him, "Yo! This wholeness that you're seeking—do you really want it?"

7. The invalid man spoke up and said, "I really need it—but, sir, when the water's stirred, I always get defeated. I am never number one; somebody faster always gets in & all I do is miss it."

8. Jesus said, "That's it. Get up and take your mat up."

9. And at that the man sat up & guess what? At Christ's request, son just leapt up, picked up his pallet, grabbed it like a simple habit & walked with mastery of his limbs like he had mentally practiced! Now the day this all happened was actually the Sabbath so you could imagine…

10 ...yeah, the Jews was crabbin', flappin' their hands, talkin' about, "We're not havin' it." They killed his groove & shut down his procession & said, "Yo! Put that mess down; it's the Sabbath, boy—you're in serious transgression!"

11 "I know my lessons," he answered back. "But the man who healed me told me to get tha steppin'."

12 So they asked, "Who the buck private thinking he a general, askin' you to break the rules, bending all our principles?"

13 But the man said, "My knowledge is minimal; it's a mystery to me"—'cause Jesus healed the man and slipped out upon the creep.

14 Later after the drama ceased, and it was calm, the Lord found o' boy in the temple promenade and said, "Word is bond; now check you out: Healed safe & sound. Go and sin no more unless something worse come down."

15 No longer blunt-witted, he took the scoop to run with it; to the Jews he passed the news that Jesus did it.

16 These Jews' already short fuse was now lit up because Jesus did thus on the Sabbath; they wanted to hit 'em up.

17 But Christ resisted 'em and said, "My Father's consistent—he's working on a daily, or you wouldn't be existent, baby, and I'm just like him, so you don't try to hate me."

18 At this they got tight fisted—ballistic from his lyrics—ticked off from his statements. And now the stakes were lifted like Cain; these brothers shifted into murderers—calling him a perjurer, circling him, lurking for his jugular. "First it was the Sabbath fiasco, but now yo, he's trying to say God is his dad! Oh, he's got to go!"

SAY WHAT?

John 5:17—One of the things that got Jesus into trouble with religious leaders was that he constantly referred to God as his "Father." That was very offensive to the Jewish people, as it was akin to claiming equality with God (verse 18).

DEVOTIONAL
Being brave enough to enter into a whole new world

If life were like a puzzle, what would you do if you had all the right pieces in place? What would be your next step if everything you wanted to happen suddenly just began to happen? Jesus steps up to a man who's been deprived of the freedom to walk for 38 years. When Jesus asks whether he wants to be made completely well, the guy finds it hard to say yes. He's gotten used to his pain and built his life around the facts of his physical limitations. The facts don't lie: He's incapable of moving on his own, he does need the help of others, he has been the recipient of very bad fortune. But Jesus isn't lying either. The guy could experience wholeness without the aid of false hopes; he could pick up the very thing that pinned him down and carry it on his own; he could embark upon a life change—but he has to want it.

Wholeness is a scary thing to pursue.

- Why does it seem easier to remain unfulfilled, wish for the best, and never have to set out for grand promises that require risk than to be filled?

- If the biggest thing you wish for in life were to happen right now, name three ways your life would be different.

- With every new breakthrough come new challenges. Name three new challenges you imagine you'd have to face as you embraced your greatest desire.

BREATHE OUT: TAG IT

Draw the facial features of the paralyzed man using verses 5, 9, and 15 as inspiration.

DAY 10
BETHSAIDA CONFRONTATION: CAN'T HOLD BACK

MOOD: COLD

JOHN 5:19-47

19 Jesus defended himself most stupendous: "I'm telling you the truth & after this consider the subject ended. The descendant of the Father's never independent; only what the Father executes I represents it.

20 "The Father loves the Son & all he's done; I'm implemented in it. But don't you get it bended 'cause you ain't seen the full percentage. I healed a man w/ a limp, and you tripping?

21 "But it makes no difference; only God can raise the dead—that's how I'm livin'.

22 "God made me your critic, handing me the last decision.

23 "So when judgment comes, the Father and the Son won't have division—equal in dimension, honor, and intention. You dissin' me, you dissin' God in my Father's vision.

24 "Now it's important that you listen: Better get some wisdom 'cause everyone who hears my words & makes a coalition w/ my Abba already has life nonstoppable; in fact, they've swapped options from the judgment to adoption.

25 "Catch these words and don't you drop them 'cause the time has come like five, four, three, two, one & boom! The dead just heard the Son. And if they heard me, they're alive again, so don't you worry.

26 "Like the Father's life is self-existent—the Son is also worthy.

27 "Built up sturdy, he's the last man standing. God is handing judgment over to him 'cause he's the Son of Man &...

28 "...don't you catch a crash landing 'cause you heard me spit these bars; see, the moment's not too far ahead when everything dead will hear my voice!

29 "Bouncing to my noise, those who made the choice to live right, everlasting joys! And to those hating: nothin' for you but damnation.

30 "See, it's not my inclination; you can call it emulation. I wait & formulate only what my Father states. You can trust it's straight; I'm just here to litigate.

31 "Now if I threw my weight, that'd only incriminate.

32 "But there's a witness on the stand you can interrogate. I know his traits: He speaks only what is true.

33 "What did you think of John? He testified, but what did you do?

34 "Your facts are misconstrued & I don't need human approval; I reviewed John's views so you could get a clue, though.

35 "John was tough like judo, far & bright like Pluto, but that light was tight enough to dance for just one night, though.

36 "But I got hotter nitro that can heat yo' mental in vitro: See these miracles the Father gave me? I'll complete those & as I complete 'em on the streets, you can check receipts; keep in mind each one done is just a cosign.

37 "My Father's signature makes it secure, but you're unsure, 'cause you never heard his vocals nor seen his contour.

38 "You couldn't detect him 'cause you don't respect the Son; I peeped your skeleton—there's no trace of God's grace, not one.

39 "You think you know the script, but why you slippin' into darkness, ya heartless—quoting Scriptures like you're the smartest but can't identify the designing artist

40 "Formally known as *Life*! Fresh right in the flesh...but my aspects you reject & bounce me like a check.

41 "But I'm the real one—see, I don't need man's endorsement.

42 "You're divorced from the love of God & of course you know that I know it.

43 "Although I was the Ambassador sent, you snored on me...ignoring. I guess if my message was impure like yours, you immature fools would be adoring it.

44 "How could your heart absorb this? You're more caught up with acting self-important than seeking God's glory; faith wouldn't come to you if I forced it.

45 "And if it don't fit, I don't resource it; but don't think my manners are abhorrent: Moses, the one you put your hopes in, he's scopin' & he'll put his words down on it.

46 "Oh, I thought you loved some Moses, but I suppose it's only incognito 'cause he wrote of me, so

47 "if you can't believe those sacred texts, what can I expect? You just got checked. Next time you step to me, better come correct."

SAY WHAT?

John 5:44—Probably the most scathing accusation Jesus ever made; here he said that the religious leaders of his day were unable to believe in him because their pride was in the way.

DEVOTIONAL

Getting on the wrong side of Jesus

No one would ever want to get on Jesus' bad side. Many assume Jesus doesn't even have a bad side, but if you explore the Scriptures, you find out some things in life even got on Jesus' nerves! Although Jesus got along with most people, the one thing he didn't tolerate was unbelief. Unbelief is more toxic than doubt because doubt leaves room for investigation; unbelief is a commitment to shut down wonder. To refuse to believe means it doesn't matter what happens—you've let rejection take up the place in your heart originally meant for discovery. When Jesus deals here with those who are committed to rejecting God's plan, he hits them hard and blunt, not holding back any words. God's plan is available and full of wonder, but you must believe.

The standoff

- Did you ever think Jesus would "tell some people off"? What's the bottom line Jesus is saying in this discussion?

- Why is the issue of belief so important to Jesus?

- How will you face areas of unbelief in your life now, knowing how passionate Jesus is about it?

BREATHE OUT: SPEAK IT

Freestyle a dramatic account of this story as if it were a scene taking place at a church service on a Sunday morning.

DAY 11
JESUS FEEDS 5,000: A TOUCH OF HEAVEN

MOOD: WEIRD

JOHN 6:1-21

1. The following period, Jesus crossed to the dry area diagonally from the Sea of Galilee (a.k.a. Tiberius),

2. where the crowds were furiously thick, tagging behind, fascinated by his miraculous signs which he did on those sickly.

3. So quickly, Jesus went up a mountainside to recline, kickin' back with his closest students for a time of brief interlude.

4. The highest feast of the Jews, Passover, would be coming soon.

5. When Jesus looked up & right in his view he saw the masses coming to see him—they found him—it touched his heart so he wanted to go & feed them. So he turned to Philip and beseeched him, "Where can we buy food, so the people can eat some?"

6. He asked the question to really teach him; he already figured out the procedures.

7. Philip was like, "Jesus, I know your heart is right, but I doubt that one might supply a bite for each one of these Israelites, even w/ 10 billion mites."

8. Then another discip'e, Andrew, Peter's brother, spake up to shed some light:

9. "This kid here has two small fish and five loaves of bread, but with this many heads, how far will that spread?"

10. Then Jesus said, "We'll have the people take a seat." There were 5,000 men alone but plenty of space for each.

11. Then Jesus reached for the bread and gave thanks for the dish and gave it to his crew, who gave to the people & he did the same with the fish.

12. And get this: All the people ate as much as they wished! Then Jesus had his crew gather together the leftovers so that none would be ditched.

13. From five little barley loaves & two tiny fishes, they added up the fragments to 12 baskets of deliciousness.

14. This was a sign. The people insisted when they saw what Jesus just did, "I swear to you that he's a prophet!"

15. They were hype about this topic & Jesus, using spiritual optics, saw that they were locked on making him their king—no stopping. So he departed, back to the mountain alone where he started to roam.

16. Later in the night the disciples went down to the sea,

17. undocked their ship, and got on, heading out toward Capernaum. See...they had waited for Jesus to get back, but they went without him because by now the sky was pitch black.

18. And strong winds began to attack and howl, making the waves wild.

19. When they had rowed the boat between three to four miles, they looked out on the water and was like, "Wow!" They saw Jesus approaching the boat, walking, staying afloat—the sight was so awesome that they were scared speechless, lump in the throat.

20. But then Jesus spoke, "It is I. You don't have to be afraid; you're not about to die." And their fears did subside.

21. Needless to say, they wanted him to come and get inside, and in no time they arrived at their destination on the other side, alive.

DEVOTIONAL
Discovering the other side of Jesus

To embark upon any new adventure, a person would normally leave room to be surprised by new experiences—but the disciples were in no way prepared for the 32-month journey when they ran with Jesus. They knew he was a man because they ate, slept, laughed, and lived with him. Yet Jesus was prone to show them another side to his nature that jacked them up. Jesus simply being himself activated a theological and social tailspin that threw the disciples off their game, constantly causing them to question each other: "What kind of man is this?" Although they never approached Jesus with that type of question, he always told them who he was. Not only did he tell them, but he also backed it up by showing and proving. Miracles were the norm for Jesus because to him heaven was not so far away, and he stayed in touch. Yet he was introducing the disciples to a brand-new world that took some time to get used to...if they ever actually did get used to the surprises of Jesus.

Surprise, surprise!

- What's the biggest surprise from God you've ever experienced?

- Name three subtle surprises we experience every day that are miracles just as big as walking on water.

- Out of all the miracles Jesus did, which one would you most like to have seen?

BREATHE OUT: RAP IT

Freestyle a dramatic account of Jesus walking on the water.

DAY 12
CAPERNAUM CONFRONTATION, PART ONE: JESUS CAN'T BE PLAYED

MOOD: TRICKY

JOHN 6:22-40

22   The next day, on the opposite side of the shore people gathered in hopes of receiving some more. They recalled that the disciples left nearly a day ago without Jesus, in the only boat available.

23   By now a few boats from Tiberius arrived shoreside near the spot where the people ate the food Jesus blessed and multiplied.

24   I think the crowd recognized that Jesus gave him the slip, so they packed up the Tiberian ships and took the Capernaum trip, hot on his trail.

25   And when they found him there, they said, "Rabbi, please tell us now—whatcha doin' over here?"

26   Unable to be veered off w/ flattery, Jesus called them dastardly: "Oh, you're haphazardly just after me, but not for the miraculous deeds but more fish platters, see!

27   "Stop trying to get fatter on things that don't matter; work hard for the meat that you feed on in the hereafter, which the Son of Man will gather and supply you with all you can eat 'cause everything he does the Father eternally guarantees."

28   The crowd all cried, "Please, then show us how you do that there, the work of God as you call it, 'cause now that's true, that there."

29   Jesus told 'em, "Fully believe in God's chosen; when you throw your whole soul in, lock, stock, and barrel, then you rollin'."

30 So they tried to cajole him: "Well, what other signs you throwing in? We want to make sure of the direction that we're going in...so you got some more works to show us then?

31 "I mean look at Moses, man—they ate manna in the desert for days; that's what the Book says: 'Bread from heaven is what he gave.'"

32 Jesus said, "Hey, Moses wasn't the one that dropped the manna—you need to supplant that title to my Father in heaven who could then and still can now and is now.

33 "For the bread of God is he who came down from heaven & this is how the whole world gets their existence."

34 At that they persisted, "Lord, evermore give us this bread; we're enlisting!"

35 Jesus said, "I am the Bread of Life, so listen. He who draws close to me will never miss his meal again—and whoever believes by obeying me first will never thirst.

36 "But tell me which is worst: I make it plain to you in open converse, and you still refuse to convert.

37 "All the souls my Father gives me don't need to be coerced; they burst toward me at first recognition & I will in no wise diss 'em.

38 "I'm on a mission, comin' down from my heavenly position not for my own whims but to accomplish the biddings of my sender.

39 "And this is my Father's agenda: That every soul rendered to my supervision gets covered & that I'd miss not one, but that all would be provided admission against the last day's judgment, catching re-composition.

40 "See...I'm-a tell you what he's really wishin': that all who get a glimpse 'n' sees the Son & believes on him will have life unending—and I'll elevate 'em when it's all finished."

DEVOTIONAL

Jesus did it God's way.

The persistent cries of a baby get her milk; the squeaky wheel always gets the grease; and the sneaky saint seems to believe he'll always get his way. From the time we learn how to make enough noise to get what we want, we begin to shape and nurture our own agendas into an obstinate force others must listen to or face our fury. But Jesus doesn't flinch at our threats of tantrum: It's his Father's will, his Father's way—period. The good news is, God the Father knows us and knows what our souls deeply need. Even though we can't "run game" on Jesus, it seems like we always try—as if we, the created, may know a little bit better what we need than the Creator. Jesus doesn't give up an inch in negotiation for our souls; it's "believe in the Son," and everything else will come into its proper place in life. We won't need to whine or kick, and God won't need to come off his throne to rescue us because he already did, through the Son.

Fully believe

- Have you ever found yourself trying to put God to a test? When and how?

- Describe the void a person feels when he demands his own way instead of God's way.

- Whose attitude do you relate to more, the people who demanded what they wanted from Jesus or the disciples who were trying to figure Jesus out?

BREATHE OUT: REMIX IT

In your own words, write out the following key verses: 27, 29, and 35. After you translate them using your words, text-message or e-mail three friends your favorite one.

DAY 13
CAPERNAUM CONFRONTATION, PART TWO: LOSING JESUS IN THE ARGUMENT

MOOD: HIGH-MINDED

JOHN 6:41-58

41 That's when the Jews got squeamish over his wording. "He said he was bread from heaven?" And they couldn't discern it. And like their ancestors in the desert, they started the murmuring.

42 "Now here he go, supposed to be Mr. Manna and ahhh... but don't we know his parents, Joseph & Mary from the Nazareth area? Man, how he goin' say, 'I came down from heaven' then?"

43 Jesus said, "Cease and settle from all this dissidence. Quarreling over me among yourselves—you're not getting it!

44 "I must repeat this elemental testament for emphasis: No man can step to me on his own; he must be drawn by my Father who sent me hence in full defense of the true penitent—standing with them, making them in-penetrate in the very end.

45 "In the Prophets it is written that 'God himself will teach each one if they'd listen.' So every man and woman that's heard the Word & learned by observing the verbs has turned, and toward me they run with the quickness.

46 "Not that anyone has seen the Father (I can't get a witness) except the Son—'cause that's where I'm from since the beginning.

47 "But hear me and hear me good: If you believe in me, everlasting life has already kicked in.

48 "I am that Bread of Life.

49 "Your fathers ate manna in the desert and are dead.

50 "But this bread I personify is truly from on high; if you take a bite, you'll never die.

51 "Right now I speak without satire or metaphor; I'm the living bread which came down from heaven for you. Anyone who eats this bread won't ever die. And that bread is my flesh, given for the world's very life."

52 The Jews, now grossed, began to get hostile: "How can this man cook up his own flesh for a hot meal?"

53 Then Jesus said, "Baby, this thing is real; you thought you was ready to deal, but off of your eyes I'm rippin' this veil: Except you eat my flesh and drink my blood, your very life force is nil.

54 "Whoso eats my flesh and drinks my blood will see eternal life bud from within, and on that last day I'll raise him up then.

55 "I'll say it again—my flesh is the real meat, and my blood is drink indeed.

56 "By consuming these I invade you, and you enter into me.

57 "Consequently, just as the Father sent me, and through him I breathe, the modus operandi is extended to those who make a meal of me.

58 "Now you see the bona fide bread from heaven—not as your fathers did eat and passed away: Whoever eats this bread shall live for ever and a day ad infinitum.

SAY WHAT?

John 6:42—Many of the villages in which Jesus ministered were small, and the people in them usually knew each other, including entire families. So when Jesus entered Capernaum and delivered this incredible message of who he is and why he came, many of his listeners were indignant because they couldn't believe this person they'd known probably since childhood (and earlier) was making such incredible claims.

John 6:57—*Modus operandi* is Latin for the typical manner in which people work or conduct themselves; in this context Jesus is saying that what's typical of his relationship with God the Father can be typical for us, too, if we believe in him.

DEVOTIONAL

The people won the argument but lost Jesus.

Sometimes God's words don't seem to make any sense, but God's words weren't given to appeal to our senses. However, God's words do make faith, and faith fulfilled in the promises of God ends up making a lot of sense. Jesus gets into an argument in the synagogue with his people about who he really is, and although the people feel they've won the argument, they lose Jesus. No earthly point of view could ever outweigh the reality seen from the other side of eternity. We can argue from our standpoint, but if we win the argument today at the cost of losing God's favor forever, then what's the use? Jesus will demand of us things we often don't understand—but trust him! Ever strive to know him and follow closely, and you'll see over time that Jesus' point of view is certainly worthy of your surrender. You may lose the argument, but you'll win eternity.

Consuming the Bread of Life

- How would you describe your life before you surrendered it all to Jesus?

- Have you ever felt as if you've tried to argue with the truth?

- How does it feel when God wins the argument? Do you still feel as if you've lost in the end?

BREATHE OUT: FLIP IT

Write out a conversation between you and Jesus where he's asking you something difficult.

DAY 14
CAPERNAUM CONFRONTATION, PART THREE: MARKING THE SELLOUTS

MOOD: THREATENING

JOHN 6:59-71

59 Right inside the Capernaum synagogue is where Jesus insight-ed 'em.

60 With this, many of his followers on the bandwagon was just about through with him: "This is a tough teaching to chew on; it's giving me a headache; I don't even know who can get through it."

61 Jesus knew that he threw them for a loop & looked to his disciples and said, "Oh, y'all trippin', too?

62 "What would really you do if you saw the Son of Man soar back to where he was before he came to you?

63 "It's the Spirit that gives you more. Depending on the flesh will strip you & leave you hopeless, broke & poor. But I assure you, the words that I speak unto you are spiritual in nature and life-making.

64 "But some of you here are even thinking that I'm faking." See, Jesus knew from the J who was the traitors & who would forsake him.

65 So he went on to say to them, "That's why I made the statement that no man can come unto me unless the Father made him."

66 After this altercation many disciples stepped away and left him vacant. They declined to even be associated.

67 So Jesus said to his 12, "Are y'all also breakin'?"

68 Then Peter answered, "Master, who could we go to but you? Your words alone are eternal and true.

69 "We a dedicated squad, down for whatever, no matter how odd—and we're sure that you're the Christ, the Holy One, chosen of God."

70 Jesus said, "Ohhh, well, let me pull your card; I've personally chosen this squad—and still one of you's a devil, straight playing the facade."

71 (Jesus spoke of Judas Iscariot, Simon Iscariot's son. This was the man out of the 12 that was to soon betray him.)

DEVOTIONAL

Jesus won't let us patronize him.

What's so alluring about false gods and idols is, you can offer up patronizing kisses of affection when you know your heart isn't in it, call it worship, and get away with it. This crime has been committed repeatedly throughout time, but when it comes to trying to rob the God of the living, Jesus won't let the caper go without notice. Jesus knows how to mark a sellout before she starts her dance of deception. The Holy Spirit always has a way of setting off the siren to expose fakeness and insincerity even if it means calling out potential so-called worshipers. Jesus knows a few real followers are better than a multitude of artificial, cliquish cohorts who wouldn't keep rank when times got tough. So he makes it easy for them to leave by exposing truths about himself they aren't ready to endorse.

Are you offended, too?

- Has God ever thrown you off guard to the point you had to check your own attitude?

- Describe the shock of a soul being exposed by the truth.

- What do you think happens to a person who gets offended at God?

BREATHE OUT: GO TO GOD

Go to God and pray for your family. Ask him to touch the people who are closest to you. Pray for God's light to shine through you so much that people will see God in your life more than they see your shortcomings or mistakes.

DAY 15
BACK TO JERUSALEM, PART ONE: HEAVENLY CREDENTIALS

MOOD: OBSTACLES

JOHN 7:1-27

1 After that fish feat Jesus walked the Galilean beat, away from the Judean streets 'cause the Jews was ready to bring the heat.

2 Now the Feast of Tents, one of the yearly Jewish events, was coming,

3 so his younger brothers came to him, tuggin': "See how you buggin'? Won't you take your crusades down to Judea & move something? That way all your disciples can participate in your escapades and do something.

4 "How you gonna try to be a savior with an unknown name? Ohh you frontin'! If you want the fame to blow, stop keeping your show on the low; take it on the road so everyone can know that you're such a mighty prophet."

5 This was their hustle, trying to gas him like ether, see 'cause they really didn't trust him, either—remember, his own kin were unbelievers.

6 Jesus swung back w/ a deep comeback: "My time's not come yet, but you young cats act like crumb rats fighting for morsels of handclaps from mortals.

7 "The system supports you, but see...me—they'd like to abort the truth that I yell, the way that I tell, the way that they failed, the evil that I unveil; I remind them too much of hell.

8 "But you go ahead. Don't wait for me. Go on, crash that Feast...last but not least; I'll go when the time is right & I feel peace."

9 So he sent them to the rally and stayed in Galilee.

10 And once they stabbed out, he took the trip up to the city on the discreet, walking the backstreets

11 'cause the Jews were on the hunt, walking round w/ a subpoena, ready to cut him soon as they seen him.

12 It appeared Jesus had the whole city steaming, buzzing on who he really was. Some said, "Dude's a charlatan." Others, "No, I think the man is good."

13 But all this talk stayed underground; no one found the guts to speak up in public—scared of the Jewish Republic. You know, didn't want to be a suspect.

14 Now midway through the festival set, Jesus surfaced in the temple, teaching the people,

15 blowing the congregation's mind as he sprinkled. "How can kid be so influential without credentials?"

16 Jesus responded, "It's simple: My samples are from the original, nonmythical.

17 "Anyone seeking to do his will is gonna feel the doctrine that I spill is accurate like digital.

18 "On the contrary, fools who bootleg theories are scary; all they cry is, 'Notice me! See me...hear me!' But a true disciplinary won't vary from the mission; the same is true, and there's no unrighteousness in him.

19 "Didn't Moses bring the Law to your attention? Why you circumventing instead of implementing? I see your intentions, lips drippin' w/ venom."

20 That's when the crowd started venting, "You's a skits-a-frantic from the clinic—who's trying to threaten you? You're surrounded by rabbinics."

21 Jesus insisted, "You numbskulls got twisted when I did just one miracle.

22 "Moses enlisted the practice of circumcision (though the origin was found in Abraham)—yet you'll still slice a man on any day you can,

23 "including the Sabbath. The same day I completely splice a man, and remember you was crabbin', waving your hands, talking about, 'We're not having it!'

24 "In that I cram to understand how you stupor at minutiae, stop using religious illusions and draw the right conclusions."

25 Then some of the ones from Jerusalem said, "Ohhh, ain't this the one they were seeking?

26 "But check him out—boldly speaking, making them look weak. Don't the priests know this is Christ himself?

27 "But the prophecies spoke on the Christ as being stealth; but we know where this bama come from—that's Mary'em son."

SAY WHAT?

John 7:4—The attitude Jesus' brothers displayed here was almost teasing and jesting…tempting Jesus to prove himself. Although it sounds a lot like a small sibling rivalry, eventually Jesus' family believed, including his brother James, who became one of the strongest leaders of the early church.

DEVOTIONAL

Heavenly credentials set Jesus apart.

The old saying "It's not what you know but who you know" runs the world. Acceptance seems to be all about who you know and who knows you. In this life access is granted to those who show the proper credentials, have the correct passwords, and are connected with the right type of people. Although those may be the standards of this world, Jesus didn't depend on man-made codes to reach out to the hearts of people (although people in his time wanted him to have some earthly credentials to give him the permission to do what he did). He possessed a higher accreditation. Because Jesus had clearance from heaven to reach into the hearts of humans, people often wanted to question his authority. One thing they couldn't ever question, though—when Jesus touched a heart, it would never be the same again.

Knowing Christ accurately

- How safe is it to have inaccurate knowledge of Christ? Explain.

- What's it like to open the door of your heart and let Jesus have full access?

- Does Jesus have full, granted access to your heart today, or are you demanding certain credentials or proof from him first?

BREATHE OUT: WRITE IT

Journal about the first time you gave Jesus full access to your heart.

DAY 16
BACK TO JERUSALEM, PART TWO: LOVE IS LOUD

MOOD: IRRITATED

JOHN 7:28-53

28 While they debated, that made Jesus plum irritated. He stood in the temple where he taught 'em & caught 'em off guard, shouting out to drive his statements: "Don't try my patience! Attempting to shut the case since you know my physical location? Y'all best to leave me alone; the quest I'm on is strictly given by him who sits on the throne. To you he's unknown;

29 "you can't even find him, but I knows him 'cause he's got my back, and I stands right behind him."

30 Once again they got grim & upset, searching for the right reason to step & break his neck—but his time was not yet.

31 And they were falling behind. The whole crowd was feeling him, saying, "Yo, he's genuine. Compare his messianic signs; there's just not one competitor & you couldn't name me one better."

32 But the Pharisees wouldn't let up. Alarmed at the murmuring of such things concerning him, the Pharisees and chief priests sent out police to arrest Jesus, killing the beef.

33 Jesus said, "I'm still on the streets, just for a minute though—when I'm good & finished, thereafter the Master is goin' back in the hands of the dispatcher.

34 "Don't try to play catch-up because you won't be able to find me; you'll just search blindly 'cause you can't climb to my paradigm, see."

35 The Jews tried to specify his message: "What is he trying to say in this lesson—that we can't catch him? Is he going to the Jews in the west, professing to the dirty Grecians?

36 "I don't know; I still got questions unanswered: Paradigms, climbing blind? What's he talking about, Master?"

37 On the climactic last day of the celebration, Jesus took a stand, crying out, "I'm embracing anyone who is in dire need of hydration—let him come to me & drink in, taking my invitation.

38 "He that believes in my offer of grace will participate in gushers of living water coming straight out of his gates as the Scripture educates."

39 But he spake of the spiritual state, the Holy Ghost promised to believers one day; but the Spirit was on wait until Jesus was received up & glorified.

40 So the crowd was wide-eyed, and those who heard the words that he cried said, "That man never lied; I'm telling you he's the Prophet."

41 Others said, "The Messiah for sure!" But some was like, "I'd like to pay homage, but what about the promise? There's no seers that were Galilean.

42 "Think back and recall what the Scriptures were saying: that the chosen one's from the line of David—no, Bethlehem is the place."

43 So the people was split over him in heated debate.

44 The haters wanted to take him and shake him down & break him, but not one hand grazed him.

45 That's when the police of the temple went back to their senders, who stressed, "Why didn't you just make the arrest?"

46 The patrol was like, "Yes, but have you heard what he said? We never heard a man like this; he made me think."

47 The Pharisees alleged, "Are you also hoodwinked?

48 "Y'all a trip—do you see any Pharisees on his tip?

49 "That's what I thought, sir. Only these ignorant sheep, people headed for slaughter."

50 That's when Nicodemus, the religious leader who was a night creeper, spoke up:

51 "Our law doesn't teach to judge a man before we know what's up."

52 With a sharp disrupt they broke into his rebuttal, "Oh, you part of his crew? Muttly number two from Galilee? Show me, B, where does the script speak of a Prophet rising from the sea?"

53 And that's how they ended the feast, split from west to east, but each ceased from debate and & went home, callin' it a day.

SAY WHAT?

John 7:52—Although Nicodemus was correct that the law of Moses requires adequate evidence before charging one with a crime (Deuteronomy 17:6), the Pharisees attempted to shut down and embarrass Nicodemus with a difficult question concerning the prophecy of the coming Messiah. (Political rhetoric is still a popular tool for dissuading truth and walking in it.)

DEVOTIONAL

The passion of Jesus won't hold back.

All those who've been overtaken by passion have had their moments of being undone, where passion takes over and they just have to follow its lead. Unadulterated passion is a fire that can be so dangerous, it must be handled properly or it could alter the course of your life. Jesus is so filled with love for his Father's will, his passion amplifies his mission to the point of shouting and making a scene right in the temple. With eyes bulging, spit flying, and hands waving to capture the people's attention, he doesn't hold back; he offers no apology or plea of excuse. Jesus stands up on the most public day of the festival and shouts out an invitation many hear, few consider sane and credible, and even less actually accept—but he does it because love won't let him wait. His same passionate call still echoes to us all today. If you're thirsty, come and drink deep till your soul is full.

Come and drink.

- How would you describe the shock of being in a synagogue and witnessing Jesus crying out to everyone in a passionate plea to come to him and drink?

- What did Jesus mean by the phrase "come to me and drink"?

- Is it worth it to embarrass yourself for the sake of getting God's message to someone?

BREATHE OUT: TAG IT

Imagine trying to explain this story to someone who's deaf. Although she can't hear, she can understand stories through pictures. Draw a five-picture story explaining the events of this passage.

DAY 17
BACK TO JERUSALEM, PART THREE: CAUGHT IN THE ACT

MOOD: MAJESTIC WISDOM

JOHN 8:1-30

1 Jesus went to the Mount of Olives & made camp.

2 Early the next day he was back in the temple, fully amped & ready to reach some—each one that saw 'im left their spot to get a closer location; as he dropped knowledge beyond education, they caught heavenly revelation.

3 Midway his illustration, here the scribes and Pharisees come with their fabrications, dragging in a lady caught right in the act of adulterous relations, smacking their lips as they dripped—they thrived off others' damnation.

4 They say to 'im, "Most popular Teacher, we caught this 'creature' in the very act of sin & it's not a rumor either.

5 "Now Moses in the Law told us how we should treat & police her—that we should throw stones and beat her & not release her—but won't you tell us what you think since you're the big-time preacher?"

6 This is how they tested him, hoping to trap and arrest him, but Jesus stooped down & wrote with his finger on the ground like he wasn't even addressing them!

7 So they persisted instead till he lifted up and said, "Let him who is without sin be the first to throw a stone at her head."

8 And again he stooped down, surrounded by those dumbfounded; he went back to writing on the ground.

9 That was it. They got hit w/ his quick wit. One by one, from old to young, the hypocrites dropped their rocks and quit. Minutes passed, and Jesus was the last man left in the pit—only with the woman left cast down in his midst.

10 Then Jesus straightened up, stretched, and asked her, "What's the deal—I thought they all had zeal; none could condemn you? None could keep it real?"

11 She said, "No one, sir." Jesus said, "Neither do I then. Go and leave your life of sin. The past is the past; don't trip—simply begin again."

12 So then Jesus turned & addressed his regimen, with a homiletical flow insistent yet agrarian, tellin' them-a, "I'm the Light of this world. I shine like halogen: Whoever follows me won't walk around in darkness stumblin', nah...but shall have the light of life in 'em."

13 So right then the Pharisees jumped at him, ready to rumble, grumbling, "Ahh! Now you frontin', talking big all 'bout yourself like you something when you nothin'—you ain't humble, man—you fumbling. Ha!"

14 So Jesus comes again with answers sharp & subsequent: "Even if I boast a bit, all my toasting's 'gitimate—ha! See, I know my origin and destination, but y'all can't figure me out, where I'm going or where I came from.

15 "Yet you same ones, judging me by fleshly estimations, can't see that I don't hate; over your state I'm still in deliberations.

16 "And if I did drop gavel on ya—the verdict would stand true 'cause my Father who sent me own ya & he's known ya since day one.

17 "Now tell me what your Bible say, son: that the testimony of two people is counted as factual affirmation.

18 "Well, my testimony makes one, and my Father who sent me makes two—so our word is bonded with validation." (Oooo!)

19 Taken back, they reacted to his response, "And where's your father?" Jesus said, "I already told you once that you don't know me or my Father either. But I'll take you deeper: If you had known me, finding the Father would be easier."

20 These were the words boldly spoken out by Jesus in the treasury at the temple, surrounded by temple police—yet no one attempted to seize the Lord or even make him cease 'cause his hour had not yet come...simply wasn't his season for leavin'.

21 So he continued, repeating, "Soon will come my season for leaving, and you'll search for the Son but won't see him and die in sin unbelieving—because my destination's out of your reaches."

22 This sounded strange to the Jewish leaders, so they entreated, "What is he, suicidal? I don't know—his words sound lethal 'cause he's saying, 'I'm going to a special place that none of you can reach to.'"

23 So he proceeded, "You're from beneath, yet my origin's celestial; you're of this world, and I'm not, so how you gonna test me now?

24 "That's just the reason that I said you all-a die in your sin—'cause unless you believe and let me in for who I say I am, each & every one of you is gonna catch a bitter end."

25 "All right, then," the Jewish leaders jumped in. "Tell us who you claim to be." Jesus said, "See...ain't nothing changed; I'm the same one since day one.

26 "And I have much to say of your generation, even to your condemnation—but he who sent me is true, so I'll just expose to the world those things that he told me 'bout you."

27 They were lost without a clue now that he was speaking of his Father.

28 So Jesus went farther: "When you've seen the Son of Man martyred, lifting 'im up through pagans' hands & slaughtered, then you'll understand the meaning of who I am—and that I do nothing of my own stance, but everything I speak on is of direct command.

29 "Man, you thought that I was single-handedly executing plans, but my Father who has sent me's at my back, so I'm far from stranded—in fact, everything I've done has been commended by his standards."

30 Standing bold in the temple & speaking these grand words, many believed on him, holding to what they heard.

SAY WHAT?

John 8:12—*Agrarian* pertains to farming (maybe Jesus was doing a country preacher thing!). But interestingly, *agrarian* can also describe the principle of equal distribution of land among people. And for sure Jesus was (and is) interested in giving everybody an equal opportunity to hear his message.

DEVOTIONAL

Jesus protects the "naked" and strips the "clothed."

In a community, elders are there to ensure people are kept safe—not in the sense of physical safety, but because of their experience in life, elders make sure we learn to live together with civility and respect. But what happens when a bunch of old men are bent on making their point to the end that they willingly sacrifice civility? As legal experts of the day the Scribes and Pharisees are busier policing people than reconciling sons and daughters. Blinded by the strain of detecting every mistake and deviation from the Law, they feel it's their right to condemn sinners. So when Jesus passes by, instead of giving him a public request to heal, the elders and watchers of the community look for permission to kill. Jesus never denies the woman's sin is wrong or even worthy of death—but the reality is, the executioners of this judgment are ready to hand it out but not ready to face the consequences of their own sin. Trying to figure out righteousness by our own standards will always leave us blind, selfish, and unable to discern the truth. Once again that's why Jesus comes as the Light: to illuminate our way and help us make righteous judgments.

The judge speaks.

- What sin in your own life keeps you from judging the same fault in others?

- If you had a chance to help this woman with your story, what would you tell her?

- If you had a chance to speak to the elders of that community, what would you tell them?

BREATHE OUT: SPEAK IT

Imagine you're at the temple that day, see Jesus writing in the sand, and can actually read his words. Write out a spoken-word piece on the words Jesus might've been writing in the sand and post it up on The Script site.

DAY 18
JESUS WITH THE JERUSALEM BELIEVERS: THE TRUTH ABOUT THE TRUTH

MOOD: BRATTY

JOHN 8:31-59

31 So Jesus proceeded to teach these new Jewish believers, "If you keep up & follow my teachings, then indeed you're my pupils.

32 "And you will know the truth in full beyond your scruples, and in full the truth will pull you to your freedom."

33 "Wait a minute," they contended. "We be them direct descendants of Abraham and never been a slave to any man, so maybe your words about our freedom was an accident. We thought you said we were bound—now we ain't having that."

34 Jesus said, "I'm coming with the facts again, so better take this serious: Whosoever practicing the sin they in's a slave to it.

35 "Yeah, you in the house for now, but slaves get in to tend to it; soon you're out the window. Where the Son is kin, I'm in for length of days.

36 "So pay attention to this phrase: If the Son sets you free, then indeed your freedom stays...never strays.

37 "I know your ways oh, seed of Abraham, but you're trying to kill me now 'cause of these words that I'm putting down you can't stomach.

38 "Now let's be honest—everything that I've seen with my Father I do admonish, yet it's highly ironic: All this hate that you vomit comes from your father's phonics; don't be astonished."

39 They didn't acknowledge that but said, "Abraham's our father." Jesus hit them harder, almost scared 'em by responding, "First for starters, if Abraham was your father, and you

were his seed, then you'd be acting like his kids by duplicating his deeds.

40 "But all of these conspiracies—you're trying to kill me just for passing on the truth to you that God has told to me. I can't see Abraham in that.

41 "You got it bent back; your performance is an exact reenactment of your real dad." They got mad at the Master, whose words stuck 'em like daggers: "We're not bastards; we all have one dad, sir, you see—& that's God."

42 "Is that a matter of fact?" Jesus rebutted, "Ain't that something when you ain't lovin' me 'cause that's where I proceeded from. I'm not here on my own; he issued the command, and I conceded to come.

43 "Now why you looking at me like you're dumb? It's 'cause my words got you hung, and your hearts are stung.

44 "I'm-a tell you where you're really from—that's the Devil. You're all his sons 'cause you love to act just like him; murder one—that was his stilo from the get-go. Of lies he couldn't let go; truth never had a foothold in him, so when he spews his venom, you see what's in him. Lies, deceit & hate: It's all his invention.

45 "And I mention the truth & none of you can get wit' it.

46 "Is it some sin I've committed? Well, where's the witness to convict it? And if I tell the truth, why do you protest & picket? Oh, I get it—as I said before, you ain't wit' it.

47 "If you were God's children, then you would hear him in my theorem. As loud as I'm blarin', yet you can't get near him 'cause you ain't his siblins.

48 The Jews started riffin', "Ain't this a blip? This kid is tripping, wild like a Samaritan & demon-driven—I'm not listenin'."

49 Again Jesus hit them, "I don't have a demon; for God I'm living. I honor my Father, and yet you hate me and you're dissin'.

50 "I have no wishes to make my own niche, but there is One out solicitin' for that top position; he has that decision.

51 "I'm-a tell you this one thing, and it's the truth so don't you miss it: Anyone who submits to my message: They won't stop living! Ever, ever…"

52 The Jews was like, "Well, I never...see, now we know you got a devil—you ain't clever—tell me, where the prophets? Where Abraham at? They dead & buried, but you say if one follows your way, they don't have to worry about dying. You need to stop lying.

53 "Are you trying to say you're greater than Abraham or the prophets right after him? They died like mortal men, so tell us then who do you think you are & who you tryin' to scam?"

54 Yeshua broke 'em down, "If I honor myself, it doesn't count. You should know by now it's my Father blowin' up my sound all around—you know, the one you call your God.

55 "Ain't that odd 'cause you don't know him from a lump of sod. But I know him; and if I said I know him not, I would have to stop—I'd be as corrupt as you've gotten, but I'm not rotten. I know my God, and my God's directions I keep on following.

56 "I know when Abraham saw that I was coming, it was something & he was glad when he saw how I had kept it real and fulfilled my summons."

57 The Jews gasped and asked, "Boy, you're not past 50-somethin' & you gonna stand here mumbling that you done Abraham?"

58 Jesus stumped 'em then, "I'm-a tell you this right now; you heard it from my mouth: I AM the I AM that has existed before Abraham."

59 This was the final straw, and the Jews were boiling hot—they got rocks to hit him with, but Jesus switched to stealth & dropped outta sight—cloaked right in the light, he stepped straight through the crowd and passed the temple by.

SAY WHAT?

John 8:41—You probably hear the word *bastard* used primarily as a name-calling device during arguments; but that's yet another example of people turning a word into something other than how it was originally intended. The dictionary says it means one born to unmarried parents—or an "illegitimate" child. In this Scripture the Pharisees are arguing with Jesus and defending themselves, insisting they know God as their father. (By the way, check out *The Message* translation of the Bible, which uses *bastard* in this very verse also.)

DEVOTIONAL

The truth hurts, but the truth works.

And the truth especially hurts when it's working out the hurts. Truth can sometimes seem cruel and heartless, especially when we find ourselves in its path of attack. Truth only hurts because it assaults those false things we've become attached to, but if we trust in truth's campaign, we'll always emerge victoriously free from the falsehoods that hold us down. Jesus said truth is to be relationally known—like a person—and through time spent relating to truth, walking with truth, maybe even contending with truth, freedom comes if we continue the relationship. Trust in truth. The only threat it presents is against the lie that threatens you most.

Pupils of truth still

- How long does it take to become free?

- Name three falsehoods in your life that truth has given you freedom over.

- Name one lie in your life that truth is working on right now.

BREATHE OUT: RAP IT

Today your assignment is to write a 10-line rap piece in "first person." Your character is: The Truth. Rap about how you (Truth) must really be known and experienced to work, how some people can't stand you, and how you've been suppressed and hidden but always stand in the end.

DAY 19
MAN BORN BLIND, PART ONE: SEEING FOR THE VERY FIRST TIME

MOOD: CRAFTY (SLICK)

JOHN 9:1-23

1. As the Master passed right on, he saw a man sitting there who was blind since the day he was born.

2. Gasping at the sight, the discip'es were quite surprised—empathizing, asking the Rabbi, "Why it's got to be like that—what did he do wrong? Or is he paying for his parents' sin 'cause blindness from birth—that's strong."

3. Jesus didn't take long to put 'em on but said, "Neither is reaping bitter judgments from sin that was sown but for one reason alone: That the works of God should be made known and shown in the life of 'Holmes.'

4. "You see, it's a must that I bust every assignment given to my trust before dawn turns back to dusk. The night's approaching, so thus I'm rushing to finish 'cause when it's clock-out time, then all assignments diminish.

5. "And in this world, I'm the brightest light as long as I'm in."

6. And when the lecture was ended, Jesus bent over & spitted in the ground & reached down and formed clay with his spit, rubbed the mud into the blind man's eyes, and that was it.

7. He told him, "Go and wash this off in the pool called Sent (that's what we'd call it, but the Lord used the name Siloam) & he did as recommended & came back with his sight.

8. So all the neighbors was like, "Wait—that's the blind beggar, right?"

9. Some said, "True." But a few spoke up and said, "That can't be; that man's a lookalike." But he said, "Nah, it's me. I can see!"

10. They said, "It's you? Then how'd your eyes become open?"

11 He said, "Scope this: A man named Jesus healed me—no joking; he made clay, rubbed it in my eyes & then told me, 'I want you to go & wash this in the pool of Siloam.' I did so & now my sight is two-O, two-O, man!"

12 They was like, "Whoa! Where is he then?" He said, "I don't know, man."

13 So they decided to take this man that used to be blind up to the Pharisees to see this 'cause it blew all their minds.

14 Now the day & time that Jesus made the mud was the Sabbath. Healing a blind man's eyes on that day could have been tragic—to some.

15 So them Pharisees, they had to interrogate: "Now how'd you receive your sight?" They just had to set it straight. The blind man made his case, "He put paste in my face, right in my eyes; I washed it out & now I can see, without a doubt."

16 Some of the Pharisees who were trying to be devout touted, "See, I told y'all this man ain't got no clout with God—he's working on the Sabbath. In the Law that's straight sabotage." But the other ones said, "Wait a minute; this is kinda odd, a mind bender—how can he do such signs if he were a sinner?" And as they discussed this, there became a division; both sides were striving, holding on to their positions.

17 So to kill the static, they grabbed the blind man and quizzed him, "You da one done got your vision; how then do you depict him?" "How do I depict him? He's a prophet in my opinion."

18 But then the Jews wasn't bending. They suspected ol' boy was pretending, so they sent in for his parents...

19 ...then began to pump them for answers: "Is that your son?" "Yes." "The one that was blind from day one?" "Yes." "Then what's the explanation for his sight? Where'd this so-called new vision come from?"

20 His parents answered, "We know that he's our son, and he was born blind.

21 "But by what means his eyes were opened, we don't know who, what, why, or how this situation went down; but go and ask him now. He can speak for himself—he ain't no child."

22 See, his parents were scared of this type of dialogue; that's why they were acting odd 'cause the leaders of the synagogue had already plotted a plan: If anyone confessed that he was the Christ, they would get banned from the temple.

23 That's why they cut the conversation off quick like Ginsu by saying, "He's old enough; ask him what he' been through!"

DEVOTIONAL

Jesus knows how to bring light out of our darkest moments.

If art is the act of taking the abstract and bringing quality, beauty, and meaningful expression to open display, then God is the greatest artist of all. Even upon the canvas of our darkest predicaments God draws the greatest portraits of faith, hope, and love. A great portrait always starts with canvas that gives strong contrast. That may be how you see your life right now: Best of times, worst of times; joy and pain; a reason to stay and a reason to run away. Don't fret—you're just facing contrast. And contrast is one of God's greatest tools used in the working of his artistry. Just stay in the frame of his will and allow him to orchestrate your complexity into the beauty he has in mind.

That the works of God should be made known

- Name three areas in your life that used to be dark and contrasting but God has brought his light and peace to.

- Name the area of your life right now that seems the darkest.

- Describe the portrait of grace God is crafting right now in your life.

BREATHE OUT: REMIX IT

Look at verses 7-9 and copy all of the action words you find. After you have a list of all of the action words, use them to retell the story using only your memory. See how close you can get.

DAY 20
MAN BORN BLIND, PART TWO: EYES WIDE SHUT

MOOD: CUNNING

JOHN 9:24-41

24   Then they called the man that used to be blind back for review number two & said, "Listen, you better give God full accreditation 'cause this Jesus is known to have a sinful reputation."

25   So he countered 'em with an answer that slammed their "hater-ration": "If he's a sinner, I don't know—I can't speak on that statement. But I know this: The physician that you hatin' just healed this patient…'cause it's obviously blatant: I was just blind & now I see!"

26   Yeah, their plan to break him down was falling to atrophy. Trying to find a fallacy, the Pharisees asked him casually, "Well, what did he do to open your eyes—did he use some kinda contraption?"

27   He answered, "You actin' like I didn't tell you just what happened. Are you gonna hear me out if I spell it out like closed caption? Or perhaps cats wanna become his disciples, too; do you?"

28   They cursed him out: "Stupid fool, please—we them real Jews. You don't even know us—we following the rules of Moses. You can follow this Jesus if you want, but it's hopeless.

29   "We know this: It's a fact that God spoke to Musa, man. Later for this loser sprung up outta we don't know where & just blew up."

30   At this the man threw up his hands and said, "Hold it; now this here scene is golden 'cause I was told that y'all all know the chosen. But y'all posin' the position. Here he opened my eyes, so he must be holdin' the position.

31 "It's known by intuition that toward sinners God won't listen. But if anyone's willin' to submit to Yah', fearin' him, God grants attention.

32 "So did I fail to mention that since time was invented, nobody's ever heard of this type of ism—that one would open the eyes of a kid born w/o vision?

33 "Now if he was not the real One, these miracles would be all frills and no skills, son."

34 Filled w/ the rage to kill, they started to grill him, "Who you think you drilling? An infidel since an infant like all these other children & you goin' try to build with us? You trippin'—get ta skippin'." Officially kicking him outta the temple to the curb.

35 But afterwards Jesus heard that he got dissed & thrown out into the streets, he found him in the cut & asked him, "Tell me now...do you believe in the Son of Man?"

36 He answered, "Sir, I don't understand. Could you point him out so that I could see him & take his hand?"

37 Jesus said, "Well, it's the man that you're listening to and looking at."

38 And in a flash the man fell flat in worshipful allegiance, saying, "Yes! Lord, I'm a believer."

39 So Jesus, seizing the moment, said, "Judgment is the reason that I traveled, breaching the heavenly chasm, stepping into this cosmos, dropping the gavel. I'm here to settle the case that those who are blind may see my face—and those with so-called sight might lose their way."

40 Some of the Pharisees that heard him as he spake were looking straight ahead, trying not to hate, knowing that he was charging them up on the low, was like, "Wait—I guess we're the blind ones. Oh, is that what you're really trying to say though?"

41 Jesus hit 'em back, tat for sarcastic tat though, tellin' em, "No need to speculate, yo, 'cause if you were really blind, you'd get special privileges & be excused for stumbling over obvious images. But you say you see like you optically got it all remedied; so when scandal hit, you'll be paying for your sins, serving full sentences."

SAY WHAT?

John 9:29—*Musa* is the Arabic translation for Moses.

DEVOTIONAL

Jesus helps us stand up to our greatest challenges with our most powerful weapon: What he has done for us personally.

Taking a stand against an oppressor isn't easy. Even if the stand has been long awaited and is justified, it still takes an extra boost of confidence to face down an enemy who has enjoyed the domination of your mind and soul. Yet Jesus loves to set prisoners free and through grace provide captives with everything they need not only to get free but also to remain confidently free. It's as if the prisoner is enjoying a table set right in the presence of his enemies. No longer does this man who was born blind have to cower under the thumb of religious leaders who choose to marginalize him due to his problem. His physical sight is given, yet maybe because of the disability of his past, he's now able to see more than most people who take sight for granted. He sees one of the greatest tools of defense against his accusers: his own story. He knows what his life was like before he met Jesus, and he's able simply to point to himself as evidence of the greatness of the Messiah.

All I know is this.

- Name two issues in your life you can point anyone toward to show the greatness of the Messiah.

- Describe your greatest before-and-after experience with Jesus to date.

- Identify the challenge in your life you're currently facing and need extra confidence to deal with.

BREATHE OUT: FLIP IT

Write out your own declaration of independence using the past pains and sins Jesus has set you free from (name specific issues and describe how Jesus has set you free).

DAY 21
JESUS THE GOOD SHEPHERD: THE MASTER'S METAPHORS

MOOD: AGGRESSIVE

JOHN 10:1-21

1 "All these shepherds is fake. Anybody sneaking into the sheep pen by the 'back gate' 'cause they can't come straight? Partner, that's a snake—well-trained in the dark arts of rape. Take notice how they can't wait to fleece the sheep & eat the sheep; watch, see how he treats the sheep.

2 "But a real shepherd comes to the gate to release the sheep.

3 "It's no secret, see, how he's known by the keeper, so access is granted—the sheep recognize his speech. He individually calls each of the bleating sheep by name; he proceeds to lead the sheep out to eat.

4 "Searching for grass that's green, his job is to feed the sheep; they stay close, following his voice...

5 "...and won't even sleep on the stranger. In a stranger's voice they sense danger and scatter away 'cause he's heinous; they can't hang with him."

6 As Jesus spoke, this metaphor seemed lame to them. He was the bee, but they didn't see how he was stangin' them.

7 So he explained to them plainly: "Let me break this down 'cause you can't see: I'm that gate for the sheep in this analogy.

8 "And all that approached me was artificial and shifty & suspicious, but the sheep refused to listen and dissed them.

9 "I'm the gate to the entrance. Come in by me, and you'll be legitimate—able to come in and go out and find fulfillment.

10 "The thief wants to steal it—kill and destroy. But I came to give them life: more life than they can enjoy in a lifetime.

11 "That's right; I'm the Good Shepherd, the real helper who lays his life down for the sheep to protect them.

12 "Hired hands don't comprehend this and get reckless. They don't own the sheep, plus they're selfish. If the wolf attacks, then the whole flock is left helpless.

13 "A hired hand is gonna go for self 'cause it's all about his own neck, kid.

14 "But I'm the Good Shepherd. I know my sheep, and they know me: We keeps it tight like cronies,

15 "deeper than sanctimony—transcended only by the way I know my Father and how my Father knows me. I'll do whatever it takes to help my sheep, even lay my life down.

16 "Right now I got sheep on the outside that I must bring in; they'll come and in sync when they hear my voice ringing. There will be one flock, one Shepherd, one God, one voice: no more mingling.

17 "My Father loves it that I'll die for the cause of you and yours, lay my life down that it might be restored.

18 "Yes, my life! Don't get it twisted: No man can lift it from me. I lay it down humbly, and I'm enlisted to come back and get it. This mission's God Almighty inscripted, so don't hate."

19 But once again the statements Jesus made caused the whole crowd to split rank and separate.

20 One side was like, "This idiot's demon possessed! His words don't make sense—why do you wanna hear him rave?"

21 But others said, "Wait; he doesn't sound crazy or flaky, and you can't make me believe the Devil just healed a blind man who can't see."

DEVOTIONAL

Jesus speaks up for his own and exposes the ones who don't have his sheep's best interests at heart.

Many have mistakenly placed Jesus in the category of being "a nice guy"; in fact, some would argue Jesus was the nicest guy on the planet. But once you've walked through the pages of Scripture, you realize Jesus wasn't always nice, but he was always loving. A loving shepherd can't afford to be nice when there are predators lurking about, committed to devouring his flock. A loving shepherd will be frequent in leading his flock, fair in guidance, and firm in correction—but toward the enemies of the flock, a loving Shepherd is ferocious. The same Jesus who promises rest for all those who come to him in sincerity also promises a fight for anyone who comes close to his flock with the wrong intentions. Don't get it twisted at all: Jesus will pick a fight over you because he loves you that much. That's why Jesus said, "Pray for those who despitefully use you" because after they've offended one of Christ's little ones, they now face a world of trouble: They face the Shepherd. This causes the flock to trust him more because we know we're safe under the care and patrol of the Good Shepherd.

The ferocious Shepherd

- Name two things you know would make Jesus angry.

- What predators of your faith would you like to see Jesus eliminate?

- How do you feel when you sense God's firm correction pressing on your heart?

BREATHE OUT: GO TO GOD

Go to God and ask him to make you more sensitive to his shepherding care. Open your heart to him and invite him to lead you, feed you, and protect you. Commit to follow his voice alone and ask him to speak to your heart today. Whatever you sense God saying to your heart, write it down and keep it with you today.

DAY 22
JERUSALEM CONFRONTATION: CHALLENGING THE MASTER

MOOD: NONCHALANT

JOHN 10:22-42

22 Now it was winter in Jerusalem, but still Hanukkah season & Jesus being Jewish was set to get his feast on, of course.

23 So he's there in the temple strolling across Solomon's Porch.

24 And the Jews came out in full force, backing him into a corner, not at all benevolent. "How long will you keep us breathless from this repressive guessing? If you're Messiah, just confess it so we can stop stressing."

25 Jesus countered their questions by answering, "I've already said that, but you're still treating me suspect—maybe the works that I do in my Father's name's a better mic check 'cause the truth's got proof in it.

26 "And you've dropped the ball from scrimmage, but you don't believe because you're not my sheep, and my voice makes your spirits scared & timid.

27 "My sheep know my voice discreetly & I'm completely cognoscente of my flock 'cause they repeat me.

28 "I give them the life that's eternal and sweet, and they'll never deplete or get weak 'cause they can't be snatched from my grip.

29 "My Father who placed them at my leadership has full ownership & you know his clench is tight, so they can never be stripped or undone.

30 "I and my Father in one are unison."

31 The Jews immediately got an attitude w/ the Son & picked up rocks to throw at him.

32. But Jesus read their actions quicker than an acronym and said to them, "I'm pulling out my repertoire—so far I can't find which miracle from God that you're stoning me for."

33. The Jews demanded, "We're not stoning you for the good works you've managed; but these antics of calling yourself God is bringing you major damage."

34. Jesus answered, "I'm only citing your inspired passages with the true semantics; what I say is not odd. Isn't it written in the book, 'I said you are "gods"'?

35. "And you know the script can't be altered, so if God called them 'gods,' then tell me who's at fault here.

36. "Now just let me get your thoughts clear. Here you've seen the one and only emissary handpicked by the King and sent to redeem; I say, 'I'm his direct offspring,' and you go off & scream blaspheme?

37. "If I didn't show & prove through these works my Father gave me to use, then don't believe me—I'd understand your moves.

38. "But since I do, it behooves you to use these clues as tools to get past your personal views and comprehend the truth that what's being done is executed by Father & Son. He's in me, and I'm in him—so we're one."

39. Overcome once again w/ the rage of fanatical men, they tried to apprehend Jesus—but nope, he slipped out of their scope and was ghost...

40. ...and made it all the way past the Jordanian coast, back to home base (the same place at the lake where John started the first leg of the race). Jesus decided to stay in the vicinity.

41. And many came out to see, saying, "John was no joke, still potent without performing miracles—but everything he spoke about this man was true to the quote!"

42. And many believed on him there and took up his yoke.

SAY WHAT?

John 10:27—*Cognoscente* refers to having superior knowledge and understanding of a particular field; in this context, it describes Jesus knowing his followers quite intimately.

DEVOTIONAL

Knowing for certain

In the arena of belief, there's a fine line—and when you cross it, sometimes you can come off as arrogant to those who still haven't found what they're looking for. But a believer who's that certain didn't concede to his beliefs because someone else said he had to; he is deeply convinced of the truth—so it's not arrogance. Far from having a braggadocio's front, you can find a place of clarity where the deep sense of knowing the truth becomes the foundation upon which you build your life. Jesus walked in this type of knowing, and many times it got him into trouble. Regardless of the pressure, Jesus never denied the truth of who he was, what he knew, and who he knew (his Father). As a result you and I can now walk in that same place of knowing—knowing who our God is, knowing how much he loves us, and knowing we don't have to back down out of shame or confusion because of who (not just what) we've placed in our lives. And the case is settled.

My sheep know my voice.

- When was the first time you recognized God's voice speaking to your heart?

- What's it like to know God is speaking to your heart—how do you know it's him?

- Has confidence in what you know ever gotten you into trouble? How?

BREATHE OUT: WRITE IT

Write out a list of the truths you're definitely convinced of and a list of truths you're still trying to understand.

DAY 23
LAZARUS IS DEAD: A TIME TO DIE

MOOD: ROLLER COASTER

JOHN 11:1-16

1. Now a certain man was sick with an illness that had him reeling; it specifically was Lazarus whom this disease was killing. Lazarus and his two siblings Mary and Martha lived in a village not far from Jerusalem called Bethany.

2. Yes, you see, it was the same Mary who anointed Christ with expensive oils and washed his feet with her hair. Here her brother was now in desperate need of care.

3. So the two sisters sent a message out to Jesus to make him aware: "Lord, your close friend whom you love is desperately ill."

4. When Jesus heard this, he remained chill: "No need to get nervous, see; first, this sickness won't end in death as the worst case. And second place, it came to serve us with a chance to see God's power blaze through his Son's face."

5. Now Jesus loved these three, Lazarus and his two sisters Martha and Mary.

6. So when he got the word about Lazarus' situation, he delayed for two more days, staying in the same location.

7. And after the 48-hour wait he told his disciples, "Pack it up; it's time to break: We're going back to Judea again."

8. These men didn't quite comprehend his tactics, so they said, "Master, last time we barely escaped disaster when the Jews were after you with stones—and now you want to go back there?"

9. But Jesus answered, "Don't you only have a limited time for the sun to shine? About 12 hours one can walk and not be blind. He can see because the sun is in effect.

10 "Yet a walk in the dark will have him stumbling after sunset, bumbling over the facts that he can't really see on his own; and when the sun is gone, it's lights out, and he's all alone."

11 He was schooling them on the low, but then he brought it home: "Our friend Lazarus is asleep, but I'm going on to wake him up and get him back on his feet."

12 So the disciples said, "Sweet! After a good rest he'll be straight."

13 But the metaphor Jesus spake of—his fate was deeper in reality's state: Lazarus was dead, and they really couldn't see it 'cause they thought that Jesus was literally talking about sleeping.

14 So Jesus made it plain this time and repeated, "Lazarus is deceased, kids.

15 "And I'm glad that I was away, if it was just for your sakes: that you'll believe—but anyway let's go to his side."

16 Then Thomas, a.k.a. the twin, cried, "Fine! Let's all go there, and we'll all die!"

DEVOTIONAL

Our friend Jesus

As recipients of amazing grace, we can be so glad to know we have a dear friend in Jesus. Knowing God is on our side gives us a sense of favor, and we feel like Joseph, who had the coolest coat (in Genesis), because we realize God has smiled upon us and shown his love to us. It's comforting to be able to call upon God and know he's right with us, closer than our next breath and nearer than our next heartbeat. Our friend Jesus who is so personal and intimate is the same Jesus who at times can even seem cold and calculated in his work with us. So you don't fall away, you must remember: Your personal friend Jesus who may not be "returning your call" right now or seems as if he's leaving you out there alone is the same Jesus who loves you deeply and isn't willing to waste any experience in your life to take you further in your journey with him. It may turn out that his answer to your plea is not only on the way, but also timed perfectly to do more than answer your cry of desperation—maybe the answer will also reveal a side of Jesus you've never known before.

I am the resurrection.

- Is there anything in your life you'd describe as dead and you want Jesus to resurrect?

- While you're waiting for Jesus to bring your dead areas to life, what are you learning about Jesus?

- How close do you feel to Jesus when your prayers aren't immediately answered?

BREATHE OUT: TAG IT

Draw sketches of the eyes of the different characters in this story:

- Jesus while he was away for two extra days
- Martha worried about her brother
- Mary crying
- The disciples going back to Judea

DAY 24
JESUS WITH MARY AND MARTHA: THE STING OF DEATH

MOOD: PAINFUL

JOHN 11:17-45

17 When Jesus finally arrived, he found out Lazarus had died and been in the tomb for four days.

18 Now Bethany was a suburb (only a few miles away) from Jerusalem,

19 and many Jews from around the way came to Martha and Mary to pay respect to their family.

20 Martha heard that Jesus was coming, so she left all the calamity of the house and went to tell him something on the road while Mary stayed home.

21 Martha spoke to Jesus in a painful tone, "Lord, if you would've been here by my side, my brother wouldn't have died, and everything would be all right.

22 "But I know that even now, whatever you ask from on high—God will grant you every one of your heartfelt desires."

23 Jesus said, "Martha, your brother is gonna rise to life."

24 Martha replied, "I know...yeah, right—resurrection day—I'll see him again at the end of time."

25 Jesus looked her in the eyes and with authority replied, "I am the resurrection and the life. Whoever believes in me will stay alive even if they die!

26 "And everyone who relies on me while they're alive won't die but will forever exist. Now do you believe this?"

27 "Yes, Lord," Martha insisted, "I believe that you're Messiah, God's Son who came to lift us."

28 After she said this, she slipped back into the house and made it through the crowd—pulled Mary to the side and secretly told her how "the Master is here now, and he wanted [her] to come out."

29 As soon as she heard that, Mary jumped up to run out.

30 Now Jesus was on the outskirts of the town, still at the spot where Martha had earlier tracked him down.

31 So everybody who was mourning Lazi's death saw Mary get up so quick that they chose to follow her steps, saying, "Yes, let's go back to the gravesite and weep with her."

32 But when Mary reached Jesus, she fell down at his feet and cried bitter, "Lord, if you woulda been here by my side, my brother wouldn't have died, and everything would be all right."

33 When Jesus saw her tears and the way the others cried, it moved him deeply inside, and from his soul he sighed.

34 "Where is he at?" the Lord inquired. They said, "Master, come and see."

35 Jesus cried.

36 "See how much he loved him!" the Jews all sympathized.

37 "Well, he opened blinded eyes," some others insinuated. "Couldn't he just keep his friend from dying?" They debated with mixed-up statements; half the crowd hated while the others just sat there and waited.

38 Deeply aggravated, Jesus made it to the grave. It was a simple cave, and at the mouth there a stone laid.

39 Jesus said, "Move the stone away." Martha, sister of the deceased, said, "Right now—from the cave? Why...Lord, by now the body's stinking from four days of decay."

40 Jesus told her, "Hey, what did I say? If you'd believe, you'd see God's glory today."

41 So they took the stone from the face of the cave where the dead man laid. Jesus lifted up his eyes, and he prayed, "Father, I thank you that you heard me.

42 "I always knew that you did, but I'm saying it for these here observing: that they'd believe that you sent me to represent your throne."

43 After he prayed, he shouted with the loudness of a megaphone, "Lazarus, come on outta that grave!"

44 And the dead man came out, wrapped from feet to face with bandages; his head was covered with a handkerchief. Jesus said, "Loose him and let him go."

45 Now what you think they did? Many of the Jews who followed Mary to the crypt found Christ that day and believed on Yahweh.

DEVOTIONAL

Watching Jesus perform miracles must've been amazing!

Actually witnessing Jesus open blinded eyes or feed thousands with a few fish sandwiches or make a sickened child immediately recover by merely speaking had to have been the most awesome thing the disciples had ever seen. Walking with Jesus over the period of three years, the disciples surely got to the point where they tried to predict what Jesus would do next. But the disciples—like everyone else—would get thrown off every now and then because just as sure as the heavens are above the earth, God's ways are higher than our ways. This is why it's so important to know the heart of God and not just the hand of God. Following God's hand may give you a sense of excitement for the present, but following after God's heart will anchor you for the future. In the case of Lazarus, Jesus didn't do what was predictable even when the pressure was obvious just to handle the crisis the way his followers expected him to. Many times in our lives God doesn't seem to come through the way we expect, but if you stay with him, you'll find out his track record is impeccable. He always brings the story out to result in glory, no matter how gory.

If you'd believe, you'd see.

- Why is believing seeing, as opposed to the other way around?

- Have you ever predicted God would answer a prayer in a certain way and he surprised you by doing it another way?

- Describe the emotions you experience when you're waiting on God to answer your prayers.

BREATHE OUT: SPEAK IT

Pretend you're writing a poem for Mary (the sister of Lazarus) to perform at a dinner. The poem is titled "When he didn't come..."

DAY 25
LEADERS REACT TO A RESURRECTED LAZARUS: POWER SCHEMES

MOOD: UNBELIEVING

JOHN 11:46-57

46 But some went back the opposite way, to the Pharisees—told them what Jesus did to see what they'd have to say.

47 Right away the Pharisees and chief priests called a secret rendezvous and asked each other, "Now what we goin' do? This man is coming hard like the truth, performing many signs, giving proof.

48 "If we try to play him nonchalant and aloof, then poof! All men will believe in him, and our exempted status with the Romans we'll lose—there goes our temple; there goes our nation."

49 But one of them spoke up, "Y'all don't even know what you're sayin'." It was Caiaphas, who was the highest priest of that year.

50 He said, "Look-a here: While y'all in fear that your fame might be stolen, you missing the opportunity—check how the web has been woven: Is one man worth our whole nation's demotion? So let's flip it and play this fool like he was the scapegoat!"

51 It was a great quote, truly prophetic, and he didn't even know it. But in the office of high priest God still used him for that moment to give the proclamation that Jesus would die for the nation...

52 ...but not just for that population—but through the ministry of reconciliation for all of God's diaspora: That they would come together one day through the wonder of his glory.

53 And from that point on they plotted to take his life.

54 So Jesus didn't walk out in the open; he played it wise and took the back streets to the countryside of Ephraim, remaining on the low with just his closest regime.

55 Now it was just about Passover, so the majority of Jews came outta the country by the droves to show up in Jerusalem to celebrate in holy convocation.

56 But instead of consecration they was concentrating on breakin' him, searching in the crowded temple with sinful intentions. "You think he's bold enough to show up for this convention?"

57 Meanwhile, the Pharisees & chief priest mentioned to those attending that if anybody saw Jesus, they'd drop dime so they could apprehend him.

SAY WHAT?

John 11:52—You should check out the dictionary definitions of *diaspora*, as many hold spiritual significance; but the one that fits this context best is "any group that has been dispersed outside its traditional homeland." Indeed, we're all "away from home" here on earth; God wants nothing more than to gather us together, bring us home, and hold us close—and Jesus is the way home.

DEVOTIONAL

Two sides of the story

It's ironic: The very miracle that gives life to Lazarus gives the religious leaders a determination to kill Jesus. Although the decision (to have Jesus die for people's sins) was formed in God's mind long before this day, the unfolding of this divine plot throws everyone else for a loop. In a time when everyone in Bethany is celebrating because a son of the village has been raised to life, others are off in a room devising a scheme to shut Jesus down. The only thing the religious leaders could focus on is how much status they might lose because of Jesus' popularity. It goes to show you—not everyone is as excited over your blessings; you may be praising while they're plotting. But go on and praise and celebrate the goodness of God because death is only a precursor to resurrection. Just ask Lazarus.

Just ask Lazarus.

- If you were a religious leader at the time Lazarus was raised from the dead, what would you want to ask him about his experience?

- How would it feel to know people are plotting your demise while you're praising God for doing something awesome in your life?

- How do you think Lazarus felt once he was resurrected and became a small-town celebrity?

BREATHE OUT: RAP IT

Now it's time for Lazarus to tell his story about his journey to the other side of the grave. Write some lyrics as Lazarus and tell of your journey and how Jesus called you back to the land of the living when you thought it was all over.

DAY 26
JESUS' TRIUMPHAL ENTRY: LOOK WHO'S BACK

MOOD: EMOTIONALLY OVERLOADED

JOHN 12:1-19

1. Now it was six days before the Passover. Jesus came over to Bethany—yeah, you know, the place where Lazarus was raised from the grave.

2. They wanted to celebrate, so they baked him a cake. Martha served the plates while Lazarus just stayed at the table with Jesus; everyone was feeling great.

3. Then Mary came in the place, with this look on her face...in her possession was a 12-ounce case of expensive oil—pure nard is what they called it. Mary broke it open and poured it out like a faucet on the feet of Jesus, wiping his feet with her hair. The scent was intense, filling the whole house like incense.

4. But Judas Iscariot, the disciple who would betray him, was on the side hatin' and tried to dissuade him, saying,

5. "What the heck she think she doing with this fragrance? She wastin' it! We could've exchanged it for a whole year's wages and helped the poor."

6. Making a case for the deprived—yeah, right—Judas was shady: watching the loot, embezzled from it all the time.

7. "Leave her alone!" Jesus replied, "She's right on time. She's doing this in preparation for my mummification.

8. "The poor will always be here, for your information, but you won't always have me here in my physical manifestation."

9. Meanwhile a large crowd of Jews found out that Jesus was in the house, so they came around to check him out, but not just Yeshua 'cause Lazarus was there, too—and they wanted to see the man who was raised from the dead.

10 So the chief priest plotted to put a price on Laz's head.

11 It was because of him that these leaders was losing cred—so many Jews were leaving and believing on Jesus instead that they had to stop it quick before it continued to spread.

12 The next day when Passover hit, Jerusalem was swoll' from many Jews up on pilgrimage who caused the news to travel quick that Jesus was coming.

13 So they took palm branches, went out to greet him with dances. As he came, the atmosphere was high voltage: The crowd shouted, "Hosanna!" The praise was hot; no one could hold it: "Blessed is he who comes in God's name! This is Israel's real King! The one who came to save!"

14 And Jesus found a young burro, and he sat on the beast's back—thoroughly fulfilling prophetic utterances spoken from way back, just as it was scripted:

15 "Daughter of Zion, you can stand fearless. Look, your King will be coming into the city, 'n' on a donkey's colt he'll be sitting."

16 At first his disciples were trippin', and they didn't get it. But after Jesus was risen in his glory, all the pieces fitted into place. Right before their face they played out, characters in God's drama of redemption penned on ancient pages.

17 Many in the crowd was there in Bethany when Lazarus was raised, so they spread the truth: "Son, until Jesus came, dude was dead for four days."

18 This was the main reason for the pandemonium; everybody that heard about this miracle was now upon 'em,

19 and that got the Pharisees and all their cronies lit. They was like, "We're losing it! Look how the whole world's choosing him!"

DEVOTIONAL

Building drama

The results of Jesus' acts begin to multiply into mammoth ramifications as God's eternal drama unfolds right before the eyes of the disciples. The words spoken by Jesus are the very formula that started it all—and now his deeds backing up his words are sending the surrounding elements into full frenzy. Prophecies are being fulfilled by the moment; religious superiors are losing their control; and the people are beginning to rise in celebrated liberty. You can tell something big is about to happen. The gates to the Kingdom of God are swinging open, and those who are close can feel the sway and bending of the gates. Imagine being in the midst of so much bustle and electric atmosphere. God has made his move, and the events to follow are cataclysmic.

Hosanna to the real King

- What would you describe as the most important, interesting part of this passage: The party for Jesus with Lazarus as special guest or the parade into Jerusalem with the children dancing and singing? Why?

- Both acts of worship (Mary's anointing Jesus with oil and the children shouting and dancing) seemed foolish to some. Why do you think some people didn't like those acts of worship?

- Do you ever feel as if your form of worship might be despised by others?

BREATHE OUT: REMIX IT

In today's passage we have two different acts of worship directed toward Jesus. Compare the difference between Mary's acts of worship in verses 3-8 and the crowd's acts of worship in verses 14-16.

DAY 27
JESUS IS SOUGHT OUT BY THE GREEKS: R.E.S.P.E.C.T.

MOOD: FINALLY

JOHN 12:20-34

20 Now there were certain Greeks there in Jerusalem, converted Jews up to worship at the feast who were in lieu of him.

21 So they stepped to Philip, the Bethsaidan from Galilee, and asked him, "Sir, if Jesus is here, can we please see?"

22 Finally getting that R.E.S.P.E.C.T! Philip told Andrew, and both of them came to Jesus.

23 And he said, "See, the time has come for the Son to blow up.

24 "But I'm-a tell you the truth: No seed can ever grow up unless you plant it down in the dirt; it has to be abandoned and hurt. But if it dies, it produces much more fruit than at first.

25 "Think in reverse. If you love this life, you'll lose it for all that it's worth; but if you hate your life in this world, then in eternity it's yours.

26 "You have to follow me close if you want to be my disciples and serve, so close that wherever I turn, you turn right on the curve. And as you serve me, you'll be honored by my Father.

27 "But now my soul is bothered. I'm closer to the edge, and the water's getting hotter! Should I ask my Dad to save me from this hour? But this is the reason I was born, and I'm not a coward—

28 "So, Father, glorify your name right now." As soon as the prayer was out of his mouth, a voice from heaven spoke down and said, "My child, I've done it before, and I'll glorify it again."

29 So when the crowd heard the sound, they thought it was the wind, or some rain, or some thunder, but others stood back in wonder and said, "It was him and an angel in conversation."

30 Then Jesus let them know, "Wait—this voice was revealed not for me, but for your sakes.

31 "And now here comes the judge, bringing judgment on this whole place: It's about to go down—for this world and for its prince who's in violation. Satan is about to be terminated!

32 "But for me, when I'm lifted up from the earth, I'll draw in every nation."

33 As he said this, he was still schooling them, giving an indication of how he was going to die.

34 So the people asked him, "Why you making insinuations about some execution? If you the Son, the Law said you'd be the one to bring revolution, and you'd never leave us. So tell us, who's this 'Son of Man' supposed to be, Mr. Jesus?"

DEVOTIONAL

Celebrity versus reality

Fame has the ability to bring the greatest revolutions to a halt. It's hard to capture the attention and favor of the masses so much so that an idea reaches its tipping point and people finally get it. Most revolutionaries gladly welcome the attention and can't wait to "go platinum," but as God's revolutionary, Jesus doesn't respond in the typical fashion to his newfound fame. Finally gaining the attention and respect of the people, Jesus begins to lay out the true realities of change: Obscurity, death, and then resurrection. He's definitely over his disciples' heads at this time—to the extent they confess that it isn't until after Jesus rises again when they're actually able to put it all together. Why is Jesus talking about dying when everyone's applauding him? It seems as if he's finally reached his goal: To get to Jerusalem and be hailed as the people's choice. However, Jesus' mission was bigger than the people of that region: God sent him to reconcile the entire planet to God. So man-made methods, mass marketing, and popularity polls aren't options. Jesus has to stick to the divine plan.

Think in reverse.

- Name three ways the kingdom of this world thinks in reverse to the kingdom of God.

- Why is the route to resurrection through obscurity, pain, and even death?

- Name something in your life (possession, attitude, habit) that must die for you to find the true joy of the resurrection.

BREATHE OUT: FLIP IT

Look at today's passage from a different angle. What would've happened if Jesus played into the temptation of worldly fame and recognition? With that in mind, go back to the passage and write out the values at stake in this pivotal moment in the life of Jesus.

DAY 28
JESUS' LAST PUBLIC OFFER: THE OUTCRY

MOOD: DRASTIC

JOHN 12:35-50

35 But he just replied, "You got just a little time to see me shine. You better walk in my lime before darkness takes your mind 'cause the blind ones—they already dying without direction.

36 "Believe in the Light while you have it with you, and you'll be the Light's successors." After this session Jesus left them, hid himself from their detection.

37 Even after all the miracles right in their presence, they still could reject him.

38 But what you expect? This is just what Isaiah prophesied under inspiration: "Lord, who has believed our affirmation? Has anyone really seen how your arm can save the nations?"

39 This is why they were skeptical and couldn't take his quote in faith 'cause Isaiah's statements were straight. The Prophet also reiterated:

40 "That their vision will be lost 'cause God would take it and that their heart will be hardened 'cause that's how God made it—so that being deaf, dumb, and blind, they couldn't turn and be healed or refined."

41 See what Isaiah was sayin'? He knew it was about the Christ because he saw his glory and then made the report.

42 And despite all this, mad crowds—even some leaders—believed in their hearts, without giving public support. They knew the synagogue would rip them apart.

43 But here's the real reason in short: They loved men's praises more than the respect that comes from God.

44 So Jesus went off on them, shouting at the crowd, "He who believes in me is really trusting in him who's sent me out;

45 "and he who sees me sees the One who gave me orders.

46 "I've stepped into your borders like light shining on disorder or a spark disturbing the darkness—all this so that those who are in the dark can depart from their abyss.

47 "So if any man hears me and still diss, that's his death wish. I'm not gonna judge him 'cause I came to save the planet.

48 "But all you who hear my message and still damn it, these words'll come back and haunt you on the last day when you'll be examined.

49 "These aren't my words; I'm quoting the One who gave me the commandment.

50 "And I know that his adages are life everlasting. So I'm just passing on the passages that he's asked me to manage."

SAY WHAT?

John 12:48—You likely hear the word *damn* exclaimed carelessly when people are surprised or upset (i.e., cussing). But folks shouldn't be so flippant with this word; it's serious business. It should only be spoken in its proper context, which typically refers to being doomed to eternal punishment. It can also mean to declare something unfit or invalid—which is the context of this verse. But let's never use this word as a curse.

DEVOTIONAL

Who do you want praise from?

I've been told that if people ever got a clear look at Jesus and saw him as he really is, nothing would hold them back from giving their hearts to Jesus in total allegiance. I beg to differ because here many see him and hear his words, yet they deny the resonance of truth that hits their souls and make the decision to reject the great Jesus openly. As to why or how such a terrible thing could occur, we find the answer right here. Bottom line as to why Jesus' own people reject him: They love praise from people rather than honor and praise from God. Could you follow Jesus even at the risk of losing the respect of people around you? Whose approval rating matters most to you—people, who you see, or God, who you can't see? If you choose God, then the old saying "Seeing is believing" can't hold you back because although you can't see your God, knowing you make him smile with your life means everything.

Has anybody believed our affirmation?

- What if no one (including the disciples) believed Jesus was sent by God to redeem mankind—what would've happened to us today?

- Write down seven words to describe how Jesus feels when he gives this last appeal to his people.

- How does it feel when people around you reject your faith?

BREATHE OUT: GO TO GOD

Go to God and pray for those who seem to hear about him every day yet still reject him. Ask God to allow your heart to break for the things that break his heart. Then make a list of friends who you desire to see and accept Jesus for who he really is.

DAY 29
JESUS WASHES THE DISCIPLES' FEET: SERVICE FROM THE MASTER

MOOD: SOLEMN

JOHN 13:1-20

1. Now just before the Passover, when everything was over, Jesus knew and took it like a soldier—that his time had come to leave this world, take the weight off his shoulders, and go back to Jehovah. Having love for his own ones who were in this world of corrosion, all the disciples were treated like his own Son. Now he's about to show them the full extent of his love that he had for them.

2. By the time dinner was done, the Devil had won the battle in the heart of Simon Iscariot's son: It was Judas who was sitting at the table, taking cues from Satan, waiting to betray him.

3. Even in the midst of the mayhem, tight situation, Jesus knew the Father had gave him everything. Still in charge of the cadence, he knew where he came from, and his destination was back to God.

4. So he got up, took off his robe, picked up an apron, and he tied it on.

5. Then he got some water, and he poured it in a basin—starting to wash the disciples' feet and wipe them off with his apron.

6. When he got to Peter, Pete was like, "Wait—and you, the Master, gonna wash my feet like a slave?"

7. "Right now you don't really know what this is about," Jesus told him. "One day you gonna find out."

8. But Peter told him right out, "The Master washing my feet? That will never, ever be!" Jesus said, "Wait a minute, P: If you never let me wash you, then you'll have no part with me 'cause I truly don't got you."

9. Peter's response was reflexive just like an 'Ahchoo': "Not just my feet, Lord, my hands and head can you wash, too?"

10. "This is something we don't have to do," Jesus told him. "If you take a bath, then you're almost clean through and through; only thing left to wash are the feet, then the task is complete—and I can see that y'all are clean. But not all of you are clean like I mean."

11. Jesus said, "You're not all clean" 'cause he knew who was scheming.

12. After washing every disciple's foot, Jesus took up his robe, and put it back on, sat, and said, "Look, can you see what I just did for you?

13. "You're calling me 'Lord'; you calling me 'Teacher'—and it's all true.

14. "Well, if this is what the Master can do, then all of you should have the same attitude and be washing feet, too.

15. "'Cause I'm setting the trend—so all you then should follow it and do what I did.

16. "Let me tell it like it is: A servant can't rank above his master; neither is the errand boy greater than the dispatcher.

17. "If you capture the truth that I rapped t' ya, acting on it will leave you in the happily ever after.

18. "Now you know that I'm not talking 'bout everybody that's here—oh no, 'cause I know the one I chose is falling faster; his actions was predicted in the Scripture that says, 'He who used to eat with me is seeking my disaster.'

19. "Now I'm telling you right now so when it happens, you can believe I showed and proved just who that I AM."

20. "I'm telling you the realness, so you gotta feel this; believe me—anyone who receives the ones I send out receives me. Those who receive me are really inviting my Father to come in their hearts, and they become sons and daughters."

DEVOTIONAL

Following through

Up to this point Jesus has accomplished a daunting task: He has obediently completed everything the Father assigned him to do. Imagine being able to stand in the category of 100-percent obedience; we could say Jesus is truly on top of his game. Yet while most would relish a moment such as this and simply commit to riding out the remaining affairs of the mission without any mess-ups, Jesus knows the same motivation that caused him to make it to this point has to be focused and practiced with even greater intensity if he's going to make it through the cross. So, fully engaged in the moment, Jesus prepares for the most difficult part of his mission by doing what he's always done: serve the ones he loves. The habits that brought you this far will keep you and take you further into your purpose. It's up to you to embody those habits and practice them until they emerge as your own culture of excellence. When Jesus stoops down to wash his disciples' feet, it's an act he's done in other expressions over and over again even though it seems so odd to Peter. Peter resists, but Jesus tells him this has always been his mode of operation—and if he can't get with this, he won't be able to walk with the Master.

Setting the trend to serve

- How does Jesus still serve us to this day?

- Has anyone ever helped or served you and made you feel embarrassed? Why?

- How do you think Jesus feels as he washes Judas' feet, knowing Judas will betray him? Try to describe the moment in your notes.

BREATHE OUT: WRITE IT

Write out seven ways you can serve people around you for the next seven days. Commit yourself to serve others as you would serve Jesus and go do it—one way each day.

DAY 30
JESUS PREDICTS HIS BETRAYAL: I KNOW WHO'S HATING

MOOD: TREACHEROUS

JOHN 13:21-38

21 After he said this, Jesus' face got harder. You could tell something was troubling him—clearly he was startled. So he told 'em, "I'm-a tell you the truth: Before tomorrow one of you here is gonna double-cross me for dollars!"

22 Then the disciples looked around in horror, doubting one another, thinking, who did he just collar?

23 One of the followers (the one that Jesus loved) was leaning on Jesus' shoulder.

24 Peter looked and motioned over. On the low he told him to find out who Jesus just busted.

25 So leaning closely on the Lord, he asked the Master who was it: "Lord," the disciple whispered, "tell me here: Who's the turncoat?"

26 Jesus quietly spoke, "I'm-a show you now; watch me close as I do this. When I take this bread and dip it, the one to whom I give it is the defector who's excluded." So Jesus took the biscuit and ripped it, dunked it in some gravy, and then he handed it to Judas who was the son of Simon Iscariot.

27 And after that Judas' disposition changed to that of a psychopath. See, as soon as he took the bread, he chose the path. And Satan entered in. Jesus told him then, "Go do what you have to do; go on and get it over with."

28 No one else was up on it, so they didn't have a clue what Jesus meant.

29 Since Judas kept the money and watched over what was spent, they thought Jesus sent him to buy some food for the poor or maybe even for them.

30 So Judas stood up with the piece of bread still in his grip, rushed out into the night...and into the darkness he slipped.

31 So when Judas was out of their environment, Jesus said, "Now the Son will be seen for who he clearly is, and God's name will be glorified as it's clearly lit.

32 "As it shines, he verifies his own light that's in his kid.

33 "I'm telling you, children, I'm only gonna be here for a little bit. Try ta find me, but I'll be outta your reach, secure and hid. Just like I told the Jews, I now teach you, too: You can't come to where I'm going to.

34 "But let me give a new commandment for you to do: Love one another just like I loved you.

35 "This is the litmus, the 'true test' that you're my witnesses—when the world sees your love for each other, they'll know you're legitimate."

36 Simon Peter was listening closely, mostly lost and inquisitive, and he requested, "But, Lord, where are you going?" And Jesus insisted this: "Where I go, right now for you to follow I can't permit; but after this you'll follow me."

37 Pete looked down and swallowed deep. "Lord, tell me what you mean: I can't follow you? You know me—I'll lay my life down for you if that's what you need."

38 Jesus said, "Will you indeed lay down your life just for me? The truth be told, before the rooster crows, you'll deny three times that you even know me."

DEVOTIONAL

Betrayal on the turn of a dime

People say circumstances can change in an instant: One minute you're in a good place with life, and before you know it, your whole world is thrown into chaos by something as simple as a visit from a friend or a phone call. The disciples would surely vouch for the fact that people change and that the decisions they make can affect everything around them. In this passage we find Jesus bringing the grim news: The movement is about to self-destruct from within, all from the decision of one man. The Scripture tells us Judas' decision was predetermined to happen, but it must've been very hard to see it unfold. Even though Jesus has full knowledge of Judas' actions, it's still a cold, shocking betrayal. What makes this moment so intense is—Jesus does love Judas dearly, so it's very hard to see him change. Imagine being Jesus and watching one of your supposedly closest friends just decide to change up on you and betray you to your doom.

When the die is cast, you've chosen the path.

- What makes you personally choose to stay faithful to Jesus as opposed to walking away from him?

- When does evil take a person over—when he decides to do wrong or when he acts on his decision?

- Describe the shock going through Jesus as he watches his close friend change for the worse and choose to betray him.

BREATHE OUT: TAG IT

Draw a modern sketch of the Last Supper.

DAY 31
JESUS COMFORTS HIS OWN, PART ONE: NO HEART TROUBLE

MOOD: OKAY

JOHN 14:1-20

1. "Never let your hearts burn out from stress—regardless of the turnout, you just rest in the fact that God's got your back. You trusting him like that? Then trust in me like that.

2. "In my Father's holy habitat are many mansions: Room for resting, no question. If it was less than just that, I wouldn't even have addressed it. Now I go to work on your addresses.

3. "And know that if I go and set it up, once the place is situated, then I'll come again. You can anticipate it—the return of the King—when I'll bring you back into my inner ring so you can be with me right where I reign.

4. "You know the journey to my domain."

5. "Now, Lord, wait—not to sound strange," Thomas said, trying to explain. "But I'm not sure we're all flowing; what you're proposing is mind-blowing. We don't even know a thing about where you're going…so then how could we know the road to this location without you showing?"

6. But Jesus told him, "I am the way; I am the truth; I am the life. Get it right—no man can come to God and reunite without me; the Father won't accept no other type, see.

7. "If you really knew me 'cause we've been so tight, then you'd know the Father 'cause we're just alike. But now you'll know him from now on 'cause he's been in your sight."

8. Philip said, "Lord, touch our eyes—show us the Father; we'll be satisfied."

9. Jesus said, "Phil, I've been with you all this time, and you still can't recognize? To see me wit' cha eyes is God personified—that means you have the Father identified. So how can you ever verify asking a question like, 'Show us Adonai'?

10 "Don't you believe that I 'n' I am in the Father and the Father in I? These words that I verbalize—they've been designed and straight certified by the Father who resides on my inside, bringing all of these works to life.

11 "Believe me: See, I am in the Father, and he's in me; we're both lookalikes. But if you can't quite conceive that, believe these works I've done because you've seen that.

12 "Now I'm telling you the truth; receive it: He that believes in me with full allegiance—these works you've seen in me—they will achieve that & supersede them because I'm leavin'; I'm going to my daddy.

13 "And in my name ask for anything, and I'll do it gladly. The Son is true to this just to bring the Father fame and also to make him happy.

14 "That's right—you heard correctly: If it's in my name, I'll do that thang; you just ask me."

15 "Now if you love me with full abandonment, then my commandments—make sure you stand in them.

16 "And I will pray to the Father, and he'll send you another companion to ever be here with you in this land.

17 "The Spirit of truth—that is this friend. The world can't stand him, understand? 'Cause they only attend to what their senses sense. But you sense him because he's in your midst, and soon he shall be right in your chest.

18 "I will never, ever leave you comfortless; I will come to you—you can count on it.

19 "In a little bit the world will see me split, but you'll still see me. Then when I rise again and because I live and exist, you also will exist and live.

20 "I insist that this is when you'll get the gist…that I, that the Father, that you and me, that we all consist.

SAY WHAT?

John 14:1—Jesus had just told his disciples that they would all leave him, and that his closest, boldest disciple (Peter) would betray him, in fewer than eight hours. This must have left everyone at the Last Supper feeling very discouraged; but Jesus came right back and told them that their relationship with God doesn't hinge upon their ability to keep it—only upon God's ability to keep us. If we believe in God like that, we should believe in Jesus like that, too.

John 14:9—*Adonai* is the Hebrew word for "Lord," an approximate pronunciation for the literally unspeakable name of God (transliterated as YHVH).

John 14:10—"I 'n' I" is Rastafarian for "I myself."

DEVOTIONAL

Jesus encourages his friends, even to the end.

Some say no one can ever make you angry (although some people never give up trying)—it's always up to you to choose to relinquish your connection to peace. When Jesus begins one of his most famous discourses on the work of the Holy Spirit, he prefaces the entire conversation with the most brutal realities the disciples could ever face: I'm going to be killed, you're going to be scattered, and you can't follow me where I'm going. However, that's just the bad news. The good news: Don't let any of this get you down. I take it Jesus' closest students are trying to grasp all of this heavy information and make sense of it all. Jesus begins the good news with this point: You don't ever have to let your heart fall into a place of turmoil, even in the face of death, division, or desertion. You don't have to fret over death because you now have eternal life. You don't have to fret over division because you're now part of a universal body whose name is in heaven and earth. You don't even have to fret over desertion because he has sent the Holy Spirit to be with you always.

Don't burn out from stress.

- Has stress ever gotten the best of you? How?

- Despite all of the bad news in the world, what makes the good news so good?

- How does a person not let the worries of this world get her down?

BREATHE OUT: SPEAK IT

Write a spoken-word piece describing your first day entering into the mansion (resting place) Jesus has prepared for you. Use your imagination—describe colors, smells, surroundings, everything.

DAY 32
JESUS COMFORTS HIS OWN, PART TWO: THE COMFORTER

MOOD: PROMISING HELP

JOHN 14:21-31

21 "It's the person who knows and keeps my commands whose love is legitimate. And that's who my Father gets intimately connected with—our love is so affectionate; I will open up my heart to them and let 'em know what's in my soul."

22 Then Judas said (not Iscariot, but the other one), "Lord, how will we know you still while the world won't?"

23 Jesus told him, "Here's the antidote: Those who love me follow my quotes. And my Father loves them, making their hearts our home.

24 "Those who don't take heed to my flow—they don't love me. I'm not telling you something I made up on my own, but it's what my Father who sent me out has exposed.

25 "All these words I spoke directly to you while we've been close.

26 "But the Comforter who is the Holy Ghost, sent by the Father in my name for all of those who love & follow me—he will correct and coach you, reminding you of everything I told you.

27 "This is what I have for you: MY PEACE, given just to ensure you...not the type of peace the world would award you. So never let your hearts be troubled or tortured.

28 "Oh sure, you've heard in my disclosure that I'm passing over, but I'll be back, so keep composure. And if you loved me, your joy would flow over because I go to the Father who is my owner.

29 "See now I have showed you the preview before it unfolds, so that when it all goes down, you can believe it's so.

30 "From here out I won't talk like this no more 'cause the prince of the world is close and ready for war. But he has no grip upon my soul; it's pure.

31 "But I'll endure that the world may know that I love my Father for sure. It's time."

DEVOTIONAL

"I am with you always."

True friends can know each other very deeply, even to the point of being able to imitate each other. We pick up the subtle mannerisms and the overt rhythms, tones, and styles in which our companions communicate—and before you know it, we've got our friends penned down, able to impersonate them flawlessly at the drop of a hat. Jesus intentionally walked closely with a small group of disciples for three years so they would catch his words, feel his flow, and be able to act just like him even when he wasn't around. When the time comes for Jesus to leave, the disciples are distraught and don't think they can hold it down without Jesus being right there. They don't know the very words spoken by Jesus are strong enough to make an impact that will last beyond eternity. Scripture declares our very existence is framed by the words of God, so Jesus—the One who spoke the world into existence—knows the power of the right words spoken can hold anything together. So the answer Jesus gives to the question "How can I survive out here all by myself?" is simple: You won't be by yourself. Jesus tells us, "Remember my words, and my Father and I will make your heart our home, bringing the comfort of the Holy Spirit to keep my words relevant and alive."

Follow my quotes.

- To love Jesus is to know Jesus by his words. What are your favorite words of Jesus?

- If you could boil all of Jesus' words down to one major sentence, what would it be?

- Identify one major struggle in your life right now and then find a quote from Jesus to give you comfort and peace to make it through that struggle.

BREATHE OUT: RAP IT

Loving Jesus means following his commands and sticking to him close. Write a rap using the acrostic L.O.V.E. Your goal is to draw the main point from the passage we read today, verses 23-25.

DAY 33
JESUS IS THE TRUE VINE: STAY CONNECTED

MOOD: PROMISING HOPE

JOHN 15:1-27

1 "I'm the true vine, cultivated by my Father; he maintains and keeps me planted.

2 "He inspects the branches, disconnecting limbs that had their chance to bring forth fruit but failed to advance...while with the same lance he's pruning up the faithful to enhance their fruit-bearing.

3 "Now it's apparent you're clipped and able from hearing the words that I've been sharing.

4 "Tarry in my presence and open up to my essence. As the branch can't reproduce fruit without being connected, you can't heat it up without my candescence; unless you abide in me, you'll be the tree with the rootless system.

5 "Listen: I'm the vine; you are the branches, children. Whoever abides in me and I in them will yield fruitful renditions because apart from me you can't complete the mission.

6 "If a man is living apart from me, he's driven, cut off, and withering: gathered like branches cast into the pit to burn.

7 "If you want to live and learn, stay in position. If you abide in me and my words abide in you, you shall find the answer to all your petitions.

8 "This is how my Father gains fame for his name: When my truest pupils become fruitful, it's the most beautiful thing.

9 "I've passed on to you the same approval that came from the Father to the Son, so in my love just remain.

10 "If you keep my commandments, then true love is maintained—just like I've kept my Father's instructions, and his love hasn't changed.

11 "I'm telling you these words that my joy may become yours and that your joy may overflow, to the flooding of your shores.

12 "This is my commandment: You shall love your neighbor more than you love yourself; love each other with the love of Immanuel.

13 "Here's how you can tell the greatest love that a man can give: when he lays his own life down, choosing to die so his friends can live.

14 "And you're my friends if you do what I bid.

15 "No longer will I address you as servants or bondsmen because a master doesn't open up to his slave—but where we've been, you've seen it all; everything that my Father has told me—I've made it known.

16 "You didn't choose me on your own. I chose you and put you on. I knew that you'd go and produce the type of fruit that'd be strong, so that what you ask the Father—just like me, he'd grant you access.

17 "So love each other for real; I'm telling you, this is my commandment.

18 "If the world can't stand you, just know that they couldn't handle me before they even had you.

19 "If you were bad, too, they'd be like, 'cool' and wouldn't be mad at you—but now they're taking stabs at you because you're from a different latitude and longitude. Since you're the ones I choose, they're looking wrong at you.

20 "Remember the seed that I've sown in you. I told you that the servant's no greater than the Master; if I was hated, that's what you're gonna get, too. And if my words only drew a few, it was well worth it—don't fall out 'cause that's what you're gonna get, too.

21 "The wrong they do stems from the fact that my name's on you, and the One who sent me they never knew.

22 "If I never came down to spread the truth, they'd have no guilt; but since I've spoken, they're without excuse.

23 "Those who hate me hate my Father, too.

24 "If I didn't do these one-of-a-kind miracles, they wouldn't even have a clue; but they've seen me manifest, and they still hate me and my Father.

25 "But now you know that what was written in their Law has finally come to pass: 'They hated me without a cause.'

26 "But when I send the Comforter back down from the Father, he will not pause. See, he's the Spirit of truth from the Father's heart, and he will testify—and never lie about the Son of Man.

27 "And you'll join him because you've been here with me when it all began."

SAY WHAT?

John 15:20—Jesus told the truth; in fact, he *is* the truth. And sometimes that means hard things and difficult revelations come to light. Here Jesus prepared his disciples (and us) for persecution, saying such injustice from the world should be no surprise. But the good news is that our true reward for trusting in Christ is eternal life.

DEVOTIONAL

Have real life now.

It's impossible to capture an author's ideas just by looking at the first word he writes and closing the book. To understand the thoughts he's attempting to convey, you have to stick with the discourse as it unfolds. In the same way, our connection with God is more about a journey than a destination. Jesus came to secure our eternity, but that doesn't mean we have to wait around until time runs out before we can ever enjoy his presence. Truth be told, eternal life has already begun for the believer, and Jesus is passionate about his followers experiencing eternal life in the here and now and not just the by-and-by. This is the benefit of abiding in Jesus, abiding in his words, seeking and finding his peace, and sticking together as close as Father and Son: We become connected to the Father just as Jesus is.

Stay in position.

- What does it mean for you right now when Jesus says, "Stay in position"?

- What are your biggest hindrances when it comes to abiding with Jesus?

- Name three ways you can practice abiding in Jesus today.

BREATHE OUT: REMIX IT

Jesus is using the parable of the vine to illustrate the importance of staying connected to God through him. Take verses 1-7 and convey the same point through a creative parable of your own (don't worry about rhyming). Here are some ideas: Online access to the Internet (I am the online connection, you are the computers, my Father is the provider); electricity giving power to an appliance (I am the plug, you are the appliance, my Father is the power), or an instrument being played by an artist and giving out sound (you figure it out).

DAY 34
JESUS PREPARES THE DISCIPLES FOR HIS DEPARTURE: WHEN I LEAVE, HE WILL COME

MOOD: FAREWELL

JOHN 16:1-16

1 "I put this knowledge in your ear so you wouldn't be offended: The truth is, the future's blended with rough times, relentless leaders with unjust minds.

2 "They're gonna eject you from their synagogues, run you roughshod like demigods: The time's coming that whoever kills you will think that he's pleasing God!

3 "I know that's odd, but they'll do it 'cause they don't know me or the Father, either.

4 "I've mentioned these prophetic items so that when the time comes, you'll be reminded. I didn't put you up on it at first because our paths were intertwined.

5 "But now I'm going back to the One who sent me down to humankind. And not one of you has been inclined to request my final destination.

6 "Instead, these things that I've said have stirred up your frustration.

7 "Nevertheless, hear this truth that I'm sayin': It's for your favor that I'm going away—because the Comforter won't come if I stay. But if I leave, I can pass on the baton on this relay.

8 "And when he arrives, he'll convince the world how to judge between wrong and right:

9 "He'll prove them of what's wrong because in me they have not believed on;

10 "he'll settle what's right because I got to my Father, and I'll be outta your sight;

11 "and he'll straighten out all judgment because the prince of this world is already judged since I came hence.

12 "I have so much to show you, but like I told you, right now your shoulders can't hold it down.

13 "But now when the Spirit of truth comes around, he'll guide you into all truth that's sound—because he's not a hound for attention; he mentions everything he hears because he's tuned to me and listening. And he'll put you up on future things.

14 "He'll keep my name glistening and bring what's mine straight to you personally.

15 "Everything the Father has belongs to me, so that's why I said that what he gets, he gets straight from me.

16 "In a little while you won't be able to see me; and again, in a little bit of time my location you will find, and you won't have to wonder because soon I goin' up yonder to my Father."

DEVOTIONAL

Words to remember

It's never easy to give bad news to people you love, yet Jesus knows the painful realities of his disciples' immediate future are too important to the greater cause to allow them to get blindsided and shut down under confusion and pressure. After he preps them by the preview of their fate, Jesus helps them look past their pain toward the reward coming from the Father: The promise of the Holy Spirit. When Jesus speaks on the Holy Spirit, his words are so colorful and filled with anticipation, I'm sure what Jesus says causes the disciples literally to crave this new era Jesus is describing to them. Thank God the era is here. You can be filled to overflowing with the promise of God's power in the person of the Holy Spirit. Just ask him to fill you today.

The Comforter is coming.

- Would you rather hear bad news and be prepared for it or not hear about it ahead of time but just face it as it comes? Why?

- Describe a time in your life when you had to go through pain to get something you really wanted. Was it worth the pain?

- The Holy Spirit is here today because of the obedience Jesus demonstrated on the cross. Can obedience sometimes be painful, and if so, how has it been painful in your life? Does obedience always remain painful?

BREATHE OUT: FLIP IT

Imagine you are one of the disciples at the table that night, and as you're listening to Jesus speak, many thoughts and questions are filling your mind. Now take verses 1-7 and write a thought or a question behind each verse that you might've had if you were one of the disciples.

DAY 35
JESUS EXPLAINS HIS MISSION PLAINLY: NOW YOU SEE IT

MOOD: INEVITABILITY

JOHN 16:17-33

17 Then some of his disciples began to wonder, keeping their voices down but saying to each other, "What is he talking about—'In a little while we won't be able find him and then we'll see him in time again and that he's goin' up to the Father'?"

18 So they voiced their pondering: "What is this 'little bit of time and then a little while again'? This is too deep; we can't understand his sayings."

19 Now Jesus knew that they were craving the interpretation, so he said, "Are you all trying to figure me out—what I meant when I said, 'In a little while I won't be found, and then in a bit of time my location you'll find'?

20 "Listen to me closely and fix this in your minds: You're going to weep and cry while the world is high—haters celebrating while you're dying inside. But watch when I change the tide and all your pain subsides: all your sorrow turned to joy overnight.

21 "When a woman's in labor, her pain makes the immediate future seem like it's against her favor. So much sorrow and anguish till the baby's born, then the sorrow is extinguished: The joy of a new baby boy in the world has turned the pain into past tense.

22 "So now you have regrets, but I'll see you again; and the joy you'll have will be full, and no one will be able to make you upset.

23 "And you won't have to question me then; you can go to the Father directly for yourself. And whatever you ask in my name you will get. Just be sure to truly represent me well.

24 "Up till now you haven't asked for a thing; but I'm telling you—ask in my name: The joy that you'll receive you won't be able to maintain.

25 "I've purposely keep it deep; in figures of speech I've conveyed all of these things. But the time is coming when I'll make everything about the Father simple and plain.

26 "That's the day when you will ask in my name; I won't have to intervene.

27 "Because you've loved me and believed that I am his seed, the Father loves you himself, and now the cipher is complete...

28 "...full circle. I came from the Father down into the world; now I'm leaving this domain, going back up from whence I came."

29 And his disciples said, "Now you're making it plain—no more metaphors!

30 "We're confident in what you said before; we don't need to question you anymore. It's settled—now we know that you were sent from the Lord."

31 Jesus told them, "You finally believing?

32 "Indeed but the hour is coming—and I want you to see this—that all of you will scatter, and each of you will leave me; but I'm not alone 'cause the Father is with me, and he'll keep me.

33 "I'm telling you all of this now so that you'll have peace within my treaty. Here in this world you'll have the type of trouble that's without ceasing, but you can be confident: It was me against the world, and I still beat it."

SAY WHAT?

John 16:33—Even though Jesus gave the brutal facts that many of us will be hated, cast out, and even martyred for following him, Jesus also gave the comforting promise that as we follow him, we can overcome all of these things simply by knowing that Jesus withstood the pain and came out victorious on the other side.

DEVOTIONAL

No shortcuts

If there were a quick-fix solution to redemption, we all would've found it. But when it comes to fulfilling the will of God, Jesus refuses to take a shortcut: The greater the challenge, the greater the reward. Cataclysmic events can't always be explained in brief sentences (especially while you're presently in them)—so as the disciples begin to take Jesus at his word and ask him what all of this new language about "going away" actually means, Jesus breaks down the entire scenario. Jesus uses the metaphor of childbirth to give the disciples a word picture that will stick with them till they see him again. But just like the miracle of childbirth, the miracle of falling in love, or the miracle of experiencing your favorite taste or your most horrible fear, you have to live through it before you can ever come close to understanding it. This is the time when the disciples are closing in on the experience that changed the world.

Sorrow turned to joy

- Why does God allow those who follow him to go through pain?

- Looking back on your most painful experiences in life, do you have a different perspective on them than before you went through them? Explain.

- Looking at experiences that have turned from sorrow to joy, was it worth going through the sorrow to get to the joy? Why?

BREATHE OUT: GO TO GOD

The Bible says all who live a godly life through Jesus will suffer some type of persecution (2 Timothy 3:12). Go to God and pray for the followers of Jesus worldwide: that we'll all endure the sufferings we must face to make it to the "other side of obedience" and that God's people will experience incredible joy as they follow Jesus through the pain to the promise of everlasting life.

DAY 36
JESUS' HIGH PRIESTLY PRAYER: FATHER, I HAVE A DREAM

MOOD: INTIMATE

JOHN 17:1-26

1. After speaking these words to his disciples, Jesus lifted up his eyes to the sky and said, "Father, we've finally reached destiny's arrival: Shine on the Son so that the Son might reflect your light in full.

2. "You've given him control over the tangible so that he could give eternal life to all whom you've handed him.

3. "And this is life in full: that they may know you, the only true God beyond human understanding, and become associated with the appropriated—Jesus Christ the Savior.

4. "While I was here, I gave you all the glory and the fame. Now I've finished the task that you gave me when I came.

5. "Oh, my Father, clothe my back with the glory that we shared before the world began.

6. "I displayed the wonder of your name to these my people. They're only my people 'cause you gave them to me, and now they're seeking you, keeping your words.

7. "And now they can't be deterred—they know that all of my giftings came from you first.

8. "I passed on to them the words you gave me, and they've received it; and now they believe that I came from you and was sent by you.

9. "I pray for them because they belong to you. I'm not praying for the world now, just for the ones that stand by my side.

10. "What's mine is yours, and what's yours is mine—and through them I now shine.

11 "I'm already stepping off of this world's stage, but they will remain while I come to you again so: Holy Father, keep them through your name—all of these my people—that they'll find the oneness that we've maintained.

12 "While I was with them in this domain, I protected them, each one that you've given me except for the one expected to sin: the son of perdition, fulfilling what was written.

13 "I'm coming back to you, but first I speak before these witnesses that in the end their spirits may be lifted with true joy that's without limit.

14 "Unto them your Word was given, and the world hates them because they're different; but they're just reflecting my image.

15 "I'm not asking that you'd deliver them from the tension, but please keep them from the evil one's tendons.

16 "They're misfits in this dimension, just like me: I'm in this world, but I can't get with them because I'm different.

17 "Consecrate them to the truth of your rhythm—your Word is the heartbeat of all that is in existence.

18 "And in the same way that you sent me here with a mission, I've sent them to the world to stand up within it.

19 "I apply myself mind, body, and spirit that they may see the truth and also walk in it.

20 "Father, I'm not just praying for these here because they're only the beginning. But I lift up those who will believe in me because of their witness.

21 "I pray that they'd all become one in sequence just like we are—so the world may finally get it: that I was sent by your command.

22 "And the glory that you've given to me I pass on to them to have that they may be one...united like the Father and the Son.

23 "You in me and I in them will bring the sum to one; when the world sees this equation, they'll know where I came from, and they'll know that you love them all just like you loved the One.

24 "Father, this is what I also want: that the ones whom you've given me stay with me up front so they can see my full glory, not just the silhouette—the glory that you gave me because you loved me before the world was set into motion.

25 "Oh, righteous Father, the world—they just don't know you. But I've known you, and these have been shown; they know that you sent me over.

26 "And I have revealed to them thy name, Jehovah, and will continue to expose it so that your love for me will clothe them; and I in them...and you in me...and they in we—back to harmony."

DEVOTIONAL

Passionate prayer

When Jesus prays, God listens. When Jesus prays, we also listen because we want to be just like him. No prayer written captures the heartfelt passion of a conversation between Son and Father as the prayer of Jesus in John 17 does. Here Jesus shares his hopes, his fears, and his dreams for the future, as well as his concerns for the present—all with a warm and honest flow. Jesus never addresses God in a distant or fearful way. This is the model of how to go to your heavenly Father and simply talk.

Father, we've reached our destiny.

- Do you find it easy or difficult to talk to God as a father? Why?

- Write out five of your greatest hopes for the future and describe them to God.

- If you could ask Jesus to pray to God on your behalf, what would you ask him for?

BREATHE OUT: WRITE IT

Journal about your hopes, fears, and dreams as a follower of Christ for the next 10 years of your life. Where do you see yourself in 10 years? What are some of your fears about the future, and what are some of your wildest dreams?

DAY 37
JESUS IS ARRESTED: SOLD OUT WITH A KISS

MOOD: PLOTTING

JOHN 18:1-23

1 After praying this prayer and saying what he said, Jesus crossed the Kidron Valley and headed with his disciples toward a garden.

2 Backstabbing Judas knew this park 'cause Jesus met with his disciples there often.

3 So Judas proceeded—played the part and led the officers of the chief priest and the Pharisees with their weapons and torches.

4 But Jesus was up on the whole scheme before it started, saw them coming, so he stepped toward 'em and asked, "Who are you looking for, men?"

5 They said, "Jesus the Nazarene." He said, "Well, I AM [he]." (Judas was on the side where the soldiers were questioning.)

6 And soon as Jesus said, "I AM," something happened: They lost their ability to stand and fell backwards!

7 So Jesus asked them again, "Who are you after?" Reluctantly, they begin again, "Jesus of Nazareth."

8 Jesus answered the whole band of soldiers, "I already told you that I AM, so let these others go here,"

9 fulfilling his words of his prayer that were spoken: "Each one that you gave me I've protected and haven't let go of them."

10 Then Simon Peter gave in to impulse—pulling his sword out, began swinging in defense mode. He caught Malchus, slave of the high priest, on the ear—severed it off.

11 But Jesus stepped in and wouldn't let him set it off: "Put your sword away! Do you actually think that I'm not going to drink the cup that my Father gave?"

12 Then the Roman soldiers and Jewish police arrested Jesus, tied his hands, shackled his feet.

13 They took him to Annas first, who was the father-in-law to Caiaphas (because that year he was the high priest).

14 Caiaphas was the same one who told the Jewish leaders, "It's better that you'd eliminate one dissenter to save our peeps."

15 Now another disciple along with Simon Peter followed Jesus: The other disciple knew the high priest, so he was greeted and allowed to enter the palace.

16 But Peter stood outside the doors till the other disciple got him on the list.

17 The doorkeeper, she looked at Peter and said, "Who's this? Are you one of his followers?" Peter said, "No, I don't follow him."

18 Both security guards and the house staff were huddling to the side, keeping warm by the fire, so Peter slipped behind them and tried to hide.

19 While inside, Annas the chief priest began to scrutinize Jesus about his disciples and his unorthodox teaching style.

20 Jesus answered, "While I was speaking out, the whole world heard me; I taught in the synagogues and the temple regularly right where the all Jews meet. Take a look: My teaching is open book; none is discreet.

21 "So why are you pressing me with these fake questionings? Why don't you go out and test those who've listened to my lecturing?"

22 When he said that, one of the policemen slapped Jesus in the face. "This is the chief priest—you think you can talk to him that way?"

23 Jesus said, "Wait; show me if I said something out of place. But if I spoke the truth and made it plain, why do you get joy out of striking an innocent man?"

DEVOTIONAL

Love in action

The fate of the ages now rests in the next crucial chain of events that take place. With the action now at high velocity, small gestures are taken as seriously as all-out threats, and an avalanche of piled-up tension begins to descend. Jesus is arrested and taken away, and he seems to allow (and even ensure) it to happen. Miracles are happening, prophecies are being fulfilled, the world is changing—yet nobody notices because the crisis has everyone on lock. Yet Jesus unwaveringly walks through this painful maze of shared hatred and slowly allows the cuts to take him. Why did he do it? For sacred love.

Drink the cup.

- If enduring pain was part of God's will for Jesus, do you think we're too spoiled when it comes to dealing with challenges in life? Explain.

- Has anyone ever betrayed you or falsely accused you? How did you deal with it?

- What's the best way to endure the pain of betrayal and still remain loving?

BREATHE OUT: TAG IT

Draw three illustrations of Peter's face:

- In the garden asleep while Jesus is praying
- Trying to protect Jesus in front of the soldiers
- Right before he denies Jesus in the crowd

Circle the picture you can relate to most.

DAY 38
JESUS BEFORE THE AUTHORITIES: TRUTH ON TRIAL

MOOD: NERVOUS

JOHN 18:24-40

24 When Annas finished, he decided to leave him tied up and sent him over to the high priest Caiaphas.

25 And outside Simon Peter stood over by the fire. So they asked him, "Aren't you also one of his disciples?" "No, not me!" He denied it.

26 But one of the personnel from the high priest's cadre was related to Malchus, the one who Peter cut when he tried to squabble. He said, "But didn't I see you out there with him in the garden?"

27 Peter denied it again, and a rooster crowed.

28 Then they led Jesus from Caiaphas's house to the palace of the Romans; it was early in the morning. And to keep themselves in line with their religious devotion, they refused to cross the governor's threshold so they could eat the Passover.

29 So Pilate came out to them. Initiating the diplomatic forum, he asked, "What charge do you bring against this man?"

30 The quorum barked back, "If he was innocent and wasn't a menace, do you think we'd storm into this courtroom to have you come and stand before him?"

31 Then Pilate told them, "Then judge him yourselves by—what you call it?—your Torah." The Jews played the political card and said, "Execution under Jewish law is forbidden by Roman order,"

32 all of this falling in line with Jesus' prophetic oracles indicating specifically the way that he would die before he did.

33 So Pilate went back inside to the Praetorium, summoned Jesus forward, and threw this question toward him: "Are you the King of the Jewish consortium?"

34 Jesus asked him, "Are you exploring the answer for yourself, or did you hear about me from other sources?"

35 Pilate retorted, "Do I look like I'm Jewish; do I look like I'm worried? Your own people and your high priest turned you in this early. What did you do to stir up this type of fury?"

36 "My kingdom," Jesus told him, "isn't worldly, not even earthly. If it was, my servants would've went to war when the Jews first tried to hurt me. No, my kingdom is not of this world's realm."

37 Pilate broke in, "So you are a king then!" Jesus answered, "You said it out your own mouth, but it's connecting deep within, ain't it? And this is the reason that I came: To acquaint the world with the truth that is plainly painted before your faces. Everyone who's of the truth can hear my voice and trace it."

38 Pilate said, "Truth? What is truth? It's just but what you make it." And when he said that statement, he went back out to the Jews and said, "I find no basis to charge up a case against him.

39 "But you know the system, it's our tradition at Passover to release one man from prison—so how about this one...the 'King of the Jews'?"

40 They all cried out with a reply, saying, "No, not this one! No, we choose Barabbas." Now Barabbas was a known thief, but it didn't matter as such—see, they could control thugs; but Jesus was too much.

SAY WHAT?

John 18:30—A *quorum* is the required number of members of an organization needed to transact business, usually a majority.

DEVOTIONAL
Picture of sin's effects

Jesus is now drinking the full bitterness of our cup. Sin will never reveal its designed intent to ridicule you and break you down—it will only advertise in the form of savage immediacy. If you ever want to know what sin does to a soul, take a look at Jesus in this passage. Denied by his closest friends because they really can't help him now, bound and carried around at the whim of his enemy, he can say nothing to stop his fate. And he's finally sold out by the very ones who once thought so well of him but who've now changed because people are fickle and follow after the advertisements of savage immediacy. If you are ever in a similar situation, sin laughs at you...mocking you because it's caught another soul in its snare. Yet this time sin unknowingly has been introduced to its match: Jesus.

The catching of sin

- What's it like when someone falsely accuses you or lies about you?

- During this time of Jesus' trial, which do you think hurt his heart the most: the denial of Peter, the cursing from the religious leaders, the condemnation of Pilate, or his own people selling him out? Why?

- Describe the shocking pain Jesus experiences while being denied and betrayed by his own people.

BREATHE OUT: SPEAK IT

Pilate washes his hands publicly before the raging mob and says he's innocent of any charges against Jesus, yet tradition tells us he died "wringing his hands" after losing his mind. Imagine you are Pontius Pilate, and you just released Jesus into an angry mob and know they're about to kill him. Write a spoken-word piece trying to justify your actions.

DAY 39
JESUS BEFORE PILATE: TRUTH IS SLAIN IN THE STREET

MOOD: INTENSE

JOHN 19:1-22

1. Then Pilate treated Jesus like he was a tyrant; he tied him up and gave him a beat-down that was violent.

2. It was real ugly the way the soldiers played it, trying to leave the sacred degraded, drawing blood with the crown of thorns they braided and purple robes.

3. And if that wasn't low enough with the clothes, they shouted, "Hail the Jews' King," counterfeit esteem from foes—and body blows.

4. Then Pilate stepped in and told the crowd that he had checked him, and now they could inspect him 'cause all that he could find was perfection.

5. After that Pilate brought Jesus out on parade to persuade the crowd with the thorns and the robes to keep up the charade.

6. When the chief priests peeped Jesus, they freaked; their beef ran deep with emotional heat. Worse than a den of tigers—crucifiers. Pilate told them, "Do your own dirt; he doesn't even have any priors."

7. The Jews answered, "We keep it raw; he can't escape the claw of Jewish Law. He's got to die—deifying self is the ultimate flaw."

8. After Pilate heard this, reality started to surface: What he had interpreted had made him afraid and nervous.

9. He was swollen, seeing the web that was woven, so Pilate returned to the judgment hall where they were holding him and started interrogating: "What set you from? Some answers need to start unfolding." But Jesus stood frozen 'cause his silence was golden.

10   Then Pilate said "Oh, you got the nerve to plead the Fifth—don't you know I can lift the charges and make your freedom a gift?"

11   Then Jesus responded, "You're not a player; you only a boss on paper. The only power you savor was given by the Creator, and besides, the one whose sin was truly major was the betrayer who went astray and sold out the Savior."

12   From that moment Pilate tried to let the atonement make bail, save face, and escape the nails on a loophole; but the Jews were cold, like hounds with the pressure, and said, "Whoever makes his own crown and scepter ain't down—he's a defector, so maybe we've found an insurrector. To us you look and sound like a Caesar rejecter."

13   When Pilate heard their rage and impatient behavior, he brought Jesus up on arraignment, sat down on his judgment seat on the pavement to see what he'd do to appease these Jews. (This was the place they called Gabbatha in the Hebrew.)

14   It was about the sixth hour in preparation for the Passover. And Pilate told the Jews, "Recognize your King; look closer."

15   The Jews started screaming, "We're not giving him credence, and we're not leaving till you execute him for treason." Pilate said, "Crucify your King? For what reason?" The Jews said, "Whose king? We only owe Caesar allegiance."

16   Then Pilate reluctantly handed Jesus into the Jews' custody, and he was rushed off to be crucified unjustly.

17   Lifting up his own cross now, he was led out through the crowds to the skull-shaped hill (the Hebrews called the place Golgotha still),

18   where they did the misdeed: Crucified him along with two other thieves while Jesus was in between.

19   Pilate decided to give the entire atrocity a theme, made a sign, and hung it on the cross. It said, "Jesus the Nazarene, the Jewish King."

20   He made the sign in Hebrew, Greek, and Latin so all of the Jews there near the city could read the caption.

21   When the chief priests saw the sign, they got mad and started ranting, "Don't say that he's our king—change the sign; say, 'That's just what he imagined.'"

22   But Pilate blew them off in an instant: "I've written what I've written."

SAY WHAT?

John 19:19—What began as Pilate's sick joke became God's delivery of a profound message. The title written on the sign that was placed over Jesus' head on the cross angered the religious leaders, as they didn't believe Jesus was a king of any sort. So instead of putting Jesus to shame, this sign further proclaimed Jesus' identity. In fact, the Romans got some missionary action going, translating the sign's message into three languages so that everyone around could witness the truth on trial.

DEVOTIONAL

True to the end

Trying to escape the truth has become a full-fledged industry today, but as painful as it is actually corresponding with our reality, we all must face the truth. Each character at this point is now dealing with the truth in a unique way: Annas refuses to acknowledge it; Peter denies it; the policemen get joy out of suppressing it; the Pharisees don't want anything to do with it; Pilate questions what it is; the other disciples are now scattered and confused because of it. Yet the truth marches on. The truth has never stopped its passage. The truth came as instructed, instructed as commanded, and commanded others to walk truthfully without trying to escape—because you can't escape the truth. This is our model: The Truth who came to be our scapegoat and pay for our escape out of darkness and back into the light.

Truth marches on.

- We have many different ways to deal with the truth; how do you deal with the truth most of the time?

- Have you ever found yourself trying to escape the truth? How?

- What's it like when you surrender to truth, even if you don't fully understand it at the time?

BREATHE OUT: RAP IT

Some believe that while Pilate's soldiers brutally beat Jesus, he never said a word. Create a rhyme expressing the thoughts you imagine could've been going through Jesus' head as he stayed there and took on the pain from the brutal beatings that should've been ours.

DAY 40
THE CRUCIFIXION: CREATION HANGS CREATOR ON A TREE

MOOD: DARK

JOHN 19:23-42

23 Then the soldiers who were commissioned to perform the crucifixion took the garments of the Master and ripped them into four sections, one quarter to each guard. But his tunic was seamless, and it wasn't easily torn.

24 So they collaborated and concluded what to do with it. "Don't tear it—we could use it," they said. Pulled out a pair of dice, shook 'em up, and threw them to the ground; began gambling for the gown, not even knowing they were a part of prophecy being played out: "They tore up my clothes and threw dice for my coat"—fulfilling prophetic quotes written millennia ago.

25 Standing near the cross to witness the horror was precious Mary, Jesus' own mother, along with three others: Mary's sister, Mary Magdalene, and Mary who was married to Clopas.

26 When Jesus looked down and saw his mother looking hopeless and that disciple whom he loved next to her trying to console her, he looked down and told her, "Woman, look: Here's your son standing at your shoulder."

27 And he focused on the disciple and said, "Look—now she's your mother." And from then on that disciple took Mary into his home, respected, and loved her.

28 Now it was over, and Jesus knew that all was finished; he said, "I'm thirsty," still fulfilling the ancient Scriptures that were written.

29 Sitting right there was a pot full of vinegar, so they dipped it with a sponge—held up the soaking sponge to his lips with a branch of hyssop.

30 When Jesus tasted the sour liquid, he screamed out, "It is finished!" And screaming one last time, he bowed his head and released his spirit.

31 But the Jewish leaders still weren't content yet; they asked Pilate to speed up the process by breaking the legs of the convicts—the truth is, they didn't want the punishment to last through the Sabbath—because this Sabbath was Passover, and they'd look bad for it.

32 So the soldiers came toward them and broke the legs of the first man; went to the other end, snapped his legs to end his suffering.

33 But when they got to Jesus, they saw that he was already dead and didn't break his legs.

34 One of the soldiers took his spear, stabbed him in the side instead; blood and water gushed out—that moment I'll never forget.

35 The eyewitness has testified, and his report is accurate. He saw it for himself, and he's letting you know, so trust what's said.

36 'Cause everything in relation to his death was confirmation of Scripture read. "Not a bone in his body was broken" was one of the ancient pictures painted by the prophet's pen.

37 And again another scribed what he had foreseen in the Spirit: "They'll stop and stare at the one they pierced."

38 After this Joseph of Arimathea who was a disciple of Jesus (but for fear of the Jews kept his beliefs in secret) came to Pilate seeking to remove the body of his slain leader. Pilate gave his consent, so Joseph went out to retrieve it.

39 He came teamed up with Nicodemus, bringing spices like aloes and myrrh about 32 keys.   [keys=kilos or kilograms]

40 Then they proceeded to wrap his body with the spices and sheets, following the burial customs the Jews use for the deceased.

41 Now to the east of Golgotha there was a garden with an unused sepulcher,

42 and the Sabbath was coming soon, so they decided to set him there.

DEVOTIONAL

Pain of death

Death is a certainty we all must face. Yet as certain as death is, the sting of death, originally ours, has been taken away by Jesus. Not only the sting, but also the grasp death once had was broken by the cross. Death might touch, but it can't hold the believer—because when death came to Jesus to grab him, Jesus flipped it all and grabbed death, hell, and the grave and took their power. Yet the pain and peril of actually going through such a process were enormous. No one else could do it. Think about the moment when the disciples, Jesus' friends and followers, are all looking from various places, paralyzed by their inability to help actually live out the words of John the Baptist in a way they'd never thought would be so painful: "Behold the Lamb of God."

Behold the Lamb.

- Has someone close to you died? How did their death affect you?

- It must have been a horrible feeling of loss and despair for the disciples to see Jesus dying on the cross. Have you ever experienced the loss of something you hoped for? What?

- How do you feel now about facing the certainty of death, knowing Jesus has taken away its power?

BREATHE OUT: REMIX IT

Choose 10 verses from today's passage and write out one word for each verse to describe the moment the verse conveys. Some examples—

- verse 26 = compassion
- verse 27 = commitment
- verse 28 = ending

DAY 41
THE RESURRECTION: HAPPY ENDINGS

MOOD: CELEBRATING

JOHN 20:1-31

1 Mary Magdalene got up early Sunday mornin', yawning, coming to the tomb & saw that the stone was gone—oh, man!

2 So she ran to Simon Peter and the one loved by Jesus to greet them, speaking, "They done took the body of Jesus away from the tomb, and we don't know where they've moved him."

3 Before you knew it, that disciple Jesus loved & Pete were moving, running to the tomb site.

4 So they both took flight, but that other disciple outran "the bishop" outright and got to the tomb first...

5 ...and stooping down, looked in, expecting the worst—but didn't burst in 'cause all he saw was Jesus' linen clothing folded up there, laying.

6 But Peter was bold, and so he came in and checked out the clothes

7 and the handkerchief used to cover his face & his nose, folded up by itself neatly.

8 Then that other disciple repeated Peter's bold step and came in the tomb, and when he saw, he believed.

9 (Although no one understood what the Scriptures decreed: that he had to rise from the dead—nah, no one understood what the script had said.)

10 So the disciples went to the rest to try to figure out what they were just a witness of.

11 But Mary was sick with confusion & remorse, missing the Lord whom she loved. She couldn't hold it in and broke down at the gravesite, bent over like she was in labor; with tears in her eyes, she stooped down and looked inside

12 and saw two angels standing, clothed in white, positioned at the slab where the Lord was laid.

13 They asked her, "Woman, why are you standing here, crying with pain?" She spoke through her tears, "Because they've taken my Lord's body away, and I don't know where they laid his remains."

14 Then she turned around, sensing somebody else at the gravesite—it was the Lord! But she couldn't recognize that it was Christ even in daylight.

15 So Jesus said, "Woman, why are you crying, and who are you looking for?" Mary thought this was a gardener, so she said, "I'm sorry, sir, but if you've taken his corpse away, let me know, and I'll retrieve it."

16 Jesus spoke her name, "Mary," and she turned toward him—could she believe it? It was really Jesus, standing there before her alive! Overcome with surprise she cried out, "Rabbi!"

17 Jesus said, "Wait—don't touch me yet 'cause I haven't ascended to the Father on high, but go to my brothers and tell 'em I am alive, and, 'I'm ascending to your Father and my Father, your God and my God.'"

18 So Mary went and told the disciples, "Hey, I saw the Lord!" And the message that Jesus gave to her for them she passed on.

19 Later on that day, back where the disciples had been hiding for fear of the Jews, Jesus appeared from like out of the blue and said, "Peace be unto you."

20 Then he showed them his scars in his hand and his side; and when they recognized that it was the Lord, they were so surprised!

21 Jesus greeted them the second time with, "Peace: Now I'm sending you out just as the Father sent me!"

22 Then he breathed on them and said, "Receive the Holy Ghost.

23 "If you forgive anybody's faults, I'll throw the offenses out. As my priests now, here on earth you'll be my representatives now; and anyone's faults you refuse to pardon is caught and can't get out—you're holding the keys now."

24 But Thomas, who was one of the twins, wasn't in the room when Jesus came in.

25 So when the disciples told him that they saw the Lord again, he said it was impossible: "I have to see it for myself, or I just won't acknowledge, yo. Not only see it: I have to touch the wounds—I'm talking the gashes from the nails and the slash in his side, too."

26 Eight days later the disciples were back in the room; although the doors were locked, Jesus just passed straight through, stood in their midst, and said, "Peace be with you!" Thomas was with them this time, so what was he to do?

27 Jesus turned to Thomas: "Come and examine my wounds. Take your hand, reach in my side; and while you do, don't doubt or presume but believe because it's true."

28 And Thomas said, "My Lord, my God!"

29 Jesus said, "You believe now, Thomas, 'cause it's something that your eyes can't miss. But the one who hasn't seen and still believes is truly blessed."

30 Jesus did all kinds of signs before the disciples' faces, many that didn't even reach these pages.

31 But these were communicated so you can believe in Jesus: that he's the Christ, the Son of God, the risen Savior. And by believing you'd have life just the way that he originally made it: eternal and real, the greatest—no other life can gauge it!

SAY WHAT?

John 20:16—Even though Mary didn't recognize Jesus' post-resurrection appearance, his familiar voice was unmistakable. And Jesus spoke one word that turned Mary Magdalene's entire world from sadness to joy: Her name. Can you imagine how wonderful that moment was for Mary?

DEVOTIONAL

God has the best surprises.

Life has a way of surprising you no matter how much you try to prepare yourself for the unexpected. (It wouldn't be called the unexpected if you knew it was coming.) If we stick around long enough, we begin to weigh the good and the bad and come to the conclusion, "Life is good." However, when the surprises of life hit you, just remember this: Life is good, but God is better than life. None of Jesus' disciples are ready for the events of the last few chapters: The happenings hit them totally unexpectedly and take away all of their hopes. Yet no one understands God is behind the entire scene, orchestrating the event—and he isn't finished until his grand finale: The resurrection! The disciples would've considered the persecution and death of Jesus "just life," so you can see how the disciples are in the mindset of just accepting what has happened and planning to move on and never get in the religious leaders' way again. But God is better than life, and he steps in and turns the whole affair around. Next time you take a hit from the circumstances of life, remember—you follow the resurrected Savior who is even better than life itself.

It's just life…or is there something better?

- How would you describe your life before you sensed the surprise of God's love?

- Name a recent surprise in life that God turned around in your favor.

- Out of all the surprises in life, what would be the greatest surprise from Jesus you'd like to see?

BREATHE OUT: FLIP IT

Take the place of any of the characters of today's passage. Write out your thoughts on the events taking place before your eyes. Be sure to use detail but don't take it to a conclusion—because the story isn't over yet.

DAY 42
ASCENSION: NEW BEGINNINGS

MOOD: HAPPY

JOHN 21:1-25

1   After this Jesus appeared again to his disciples at the Sea of Tiberias. This is how it happened:

2   It was about seven of the brethren—Pete, Tommy, Nate, James, John, and two others gathering...

3   ...you know, just chilling. Peter said to them, "I'm-a go fishing." They decided to go with him and got into the boat and floated on it all night. But they came back empty-handed; didn't even catch a bite.

4   And at the break of dawn Jesus was standing on the shore, but it was like they couldn't recognize him anymore.

5   He said, "Children, good morning. Have you caught any meat?" They said, "Naw."

6   He said, "Then cast your nets on the right side of your ship and see." They tried it out (what the heck, black) but this time caught so many fish they couldn't pull the net back.

7   That beloved student knew what he suspected. He leaned over to Peter and said, "That's the Lord, man—you know his methods!" When Simon Peter heard that it was Jesus, he just grabbed his coat, threw it back on, 'n' jumped in the deep & swam in to see him.

8   But everybody else was thinking 'bout those fish; it was only a hundred yards to pull them in, so they stayed in the little ship.

9   And soon as they set to shore, they looked up and saw a warm fire roaring with fish and bread already cooking on it.

10 Jesus said, "Go on; get the fish you just caught and throw them on these briquettes."

11 Peter went over and joined in pulling the net up out the sea; that mug was full of big fish—about a hundred and fifty-three! And the trip was that the net didn't rip.

12 Jesus said, "Come and get it." But none of the disciples dared risk it by acting curious, popping off at the lip, like asking, "Who you is?" They knew it was the Lord in their midst.

13 Then Jesus reached for the bread and gave thanks for the dish, gave it to the discples, and did the same with the fish.

14 Now this was the third time Jesus did this, showing that he was alive to disciples after being risen from the dead.

15 And when they finished breakfast, Jesus looked to Peter and said, "Simon, son of Jonas, do you love me the most?" Peter told him, "Umm, I got love for you, Lord...you know." Jesus said, "Then feed my little lambs from the fold."

16 Then Jesus said it over: "Simon, Jonas' son, do you love me? Come on." Peter said, "Yes, Lord! Y...y...you know my love is strong." Jesus said, "Then feed my sheep before they starve."

17 Once more Jesus pressed him at the core. He said, "Simon, the big and bad one, yeah you, Jonas' son. But do you even love me some?" By now Pete was overcome 'cause Jesus fronted him in front of everyone. Peter said, "Look at me: You know the sum. You know that my love runs deep." Jesus said, "Shhh. Then feed my sheep.

18 "Listen to me: I've known you from the beginning, Pete. When you were a shorty, you was mad haughty! You used to grab your coat, put it on, and go wherever you wanted. But tradewinds have a way of switching the arrangement. And when you get old, someone else will change you and take you places that you ain't with."

19 He said this, giving Peter a hint about his future and the events in which his own death would honor God and be glorious. And when he had spoken this, he said to Peter, "Follow me."

20 But Peter turned and looked and noticed his other disciple who Jesus loved following both of them. (It was the same one who leaned on Jesus, asking, "Who was the turncoat then?")

21 Peter saw him and asked, "But, Lord, what about this man?"

22 Jesus said, "Now, Peter, if I wanted him to stay alive 'til I came, what is that to you, man? I want you pursuing me."

23 Now see, that's how the rumor took flight: Everybody thought that that disciple would never die, yet Jesus didn't say the boy would never, ever die; he just said, "If I wanted him to be alive till I arrived, what's it to you?"

24 This is that disciple who's talking to you. I seen it all happen, wrote it down, and we know it's all true.

25 And this is just the surface; I mean, there's so many other things that Jesus did that I had to limit it—'cause if it all had been written down for you to look, the whole world wouldn't be able to contain the books.

SAY WHAT?

John 21:13—It's interesting that John notes the manner in which Jesus served his disciples this meal; it's very similar to the manner in which the Last Supper was served. But Jesus' actions here strongly indicate the importance of doing life in the context of community, not just church. See, Jesus wasn't giving communion; Jesus was just eating a meal with his friends. And because he had done this so many times before with them, they without a doubt knew that this was the "real" Jesus in their midst.

DEVOTIONAL

All the chances you need

From our viewpoint, time seems as if everything revolves in cycles—and we've actually gotten that one right. From the beginning of his creation, God designed all things to revolve in cycles: Winter, spring, summer, and fall; darkness to light to darkness back to light. Yet when it comes to our walk with God, we're often tricked by the lies of the Enemy and think it's all over once we mess up. But God is the God of second, third, and however many chances you need to get to know him while you're alive. This is where it all begins again for Peter and the disciples: Outside by the sea Jesus comes into their world, where they are, and offers them something better. Every cycle of life you go through, always remember Jesus will be there and will always have something better to offer you.

Follow me...again

- How many times have you sensed God giving you another chance at walking with him, to receive something better?

- Although we live through cycles, each time we make a revolution (full circle), we grow. How have you grown in these last 42 days as you've journeyed through the book of John?

- If someone asks you what your favorite part of the book of John is, which story will you tell her?

BREATHE OUT: GO TO GOD

Go to God and thank him for this journey through the book of John. Make a fresh commitment to following Jesus and make a commitment to revisit what he's revealed to you through this journey. Commit to sharing what you discovered with two other people and pray for them— that they'll also take this journey.

After bizarre events at their New York concert, P.O.D. must decipher mysterious visions and battle evil forces to locate "The Chosen." Armed with super powers, Sunny, Wuv, Traa, and Marcos must fight alien Xenophon warriors and prevent the mysterious being, known only as The Soul Shredder, from getting to The Chosen first. Saving the world was never so tough—or so crucial!

P.O.D. The Nexus
Matt Broome
RETAIL $14.99
ISBN 978-0-310-71638-9

Visit www.invertbooks.com or your local bookstore.